Birth of God

By: Eric Kikkert

<u>Dedication</u>

Dedicated to Jesus Christ and my True Love.

Dedicated to all that exist not just human,
but to all life everywhere, past, present and future.
May you learn to love life.

There are some things you can tell a person and they will learn.
There are some things you can show a person and they will learn.
There are some things you must experience yourself.

I wish I may, I wish I might, I wish upon this starry night.
For all that is, with all my might, with all the light of stars so bright.
For true love to shine tonight, upon us all forever bright.
Upon the world so full of tears, to you it shines so deeply here.
To give to you this treasured gift, the truest love that exists.

Within thy soul, a hero's light,
flows with all, true loves might.

Cross my heart and hope to live.
A life beside the one I give.
All the love I hold within.
Eternal I am again.
Forever yours till the end.

God's love is not a competition!

Table of Contents

PART 3: The Science...

AUTHOR'S NOTE

Understanding the concepts within requires a basic understanding of physics, knowing that each structure has a principle to be defined and that physics is the form with which the phenomenon is explained for understanding. Know that this information is defined further by Quantum Physics using a particle model called Particle Progression. It is not God's will for life to be ignorant. Nor is it God's will to be considered magic under any terms. When you ask God a question, God being an "All Knowing" entity that you will, if you have the ability to both ask and understand, will in fact, get an answer. Even if that question is "how was God born?".

The contained information is designed to explain not just to the well versed but to all. It may appear complex but is in actuality very simple. The constructs may take a moment to put together but the structures are rooted in the most basic fundamental structures that exist. It is my hope to provide for all that means of understanding so that we all may walk in the light.

This information is not provided to present an air of correctness to any one religious practice and that while Catholic practice identifies the collective consciousness, it like all practices remain incomplete and this is identified by the immoralities, misconceptions and lack of information to express the reasons for which those structures are as they are. For instance, consider Buddhism, which maintains a great understanding of sanctity and sanctuary towards all life. It lacks the information to explain why you may become that life or how the energy of the soul moves from one vessel to another. So while each religious practice includes some form of understanding, they lack others and remain incomplete for they do not hold true morality, true sanctity, true sanctuary.

In order to fully grasp that which is God you must use all of what is God, just as to understand all that is existence you must use all of existence. The mind tends to only use just a portion of these concepts and as such only holds portions of the truth at one time. So to understand all that is you, you must use all that is you and the same is applied to religion, in order to understand all that is religion you must use all that is religion. While we attempt to break down and piece together the many parts, this is where the truth unfolds but in order to do this we must endeavor to refine ourselves and in doing so we will identify more and more truths.

Religion should be founded not just under the concept of the highest, most pure and refined love, morality, sanctity and sanctuary. It should also be founded by logic and reason and this is something science provides and as such we not only obtain a greater understanding of these structures but we can provide a depth to our existence so we may obtain absolute truth.

Everything that exists is both separate and connected, in one form or another and often in many forms we are woven into each other to create all that is. Big things are made of little things and to discard any part of those things we discard the whole. Every part of it must be understood otherwise the whole will not be understood. To discard even a single piece of that understanding creates a misunderstanding.

Faith is for those without truth, for when truth is obtained faith is not required.

FOREWORD

Many folks, not just in a religious field but scientific field find themselves in conflict. That one is right and the other is wrong. They quarrel and contradict each other on repeat in a way that divides those who walk those paths. This itself is improper and that science is but a means to define the phenomenon itself in a way that the mind can understand using a structure we refer to as physics which is created using logic and reason through experimentation to produce an understanding of our existence.

We are not meant to be in conflict and both religion and science are in reality intertwined, even if we do not want them to be. Through scientific knowledge a greater understanding of the phenomenon, that which is God can be obtained and a greater path can be forged into the future. That by using scientific knowledge we can obtain not just greater truth through this understanding but even obtain a means to prove it.

So we look to the future with the hopes of unity between science and religion as we deepen our understanding of existence so that we may create paradise on earth as it is in heaven. May you grasp it with all your heart and soul.

Remember that 2000 years ago the words and their meanings were used and represented by different definitions and concepts and even intent then it is today. It is very important that what is written is understood properly for many generations to come. To that end you must understand that misconceptions occur and may even be purposely created through the augmentation of the spoken word over generations as they change the definitions of the spoken words used in any and all languages.

It also remains possible that the usage of that which is written here may be taken out of context in an attempt to augment how a word is interpreted often referred to as semantic shift, four common types of changes are broadening, narrowing, amelioration, and pejoration. For whatever reason they may be doing so this can be an immorality and this immorality can be expressed by educated consent. You were not educated and thus did not consent to the manipulation of the spoken word to be used against you which may deter your understanding. The same is true for those that state you are not allowed to read or know the information within, those that do this wish to maintain your ignorance by refusing to permit educated consent and this is a means to control and manipulate the information you have. Remember this and know it for the truth it is. God's will is not for you to be ignorant. God does not seek obedience or fear, God seeks love and that you should choose to do because it is righteous, because it is moral.

God Bless You.

God Bless You All.

And God Bless Myself.

I Love You.

I Love You All.

And I Love Myself.

PART 1:

In the End, it Begins...

THE END

In the end, is when it begins, you may consider this a paradox and this may be true but it starts as the first existence that held life ends. God is a collection of consciousness from a time where life existed and ended. In these moments as that existence ended God was born. The cosmos life came to an end and every life form everywhere becomes the source everlasting.

This collection is formed by force as the cosmos collapses upon itself gathering all that exists into one. The consciousness of every life form, the energies from all inorganic and organic matter collide into a single point so incredibly fast that no death signal could be passed from the body to the mind. A force quite literally so incredible and massive our minds have quite a difficult time grasping. If you consider how fast light travels from your spine to your brain, the entire cosmos itself fell upon itself many times faster. So fast that the brain and body had no idea what had happened. No death signal could be passed to the brain and so the consciousness of all the life that existed entered that single point right beside everything else.

Each consciousness at this point becomes one, not just organic matter but also inorganic matter, energies and particles of all forms of density residing together. There was no suffering from this and it is important to remember that it occurred so fast, so incredibly fast the very signals from the body could not reach the brain which means all those nerves which pass signals of pain never activated. This itself seems horrific and frightening but take at least some comfort in knowing that truth.

Our understanding of what life is and how it may exist is still somewhat infantile. Life can be formed under any structure of density and volume. It resides in so many ways across existence it seems to most to be inconceivable. All the knowledge and understandings of those forms of life, all the collective knowledge that existed from every culture and form of life also became one. Every form of literature, art, science, religion, that had ever been resided side by side as one.

To understand how this can occur you must understand that force itself is and can be infinite. It is literally the only truly infinite physical source that exists. It is also important to understand that all that is, has been or will ever be, exists because force exists and this includes God.

Many physicist speculate as to how this collapse could occur but it stands to reason that the force presented outwards from the center of the quantum explosion was insufficient to maintain an outward expansion indefinitely and that the density of the space outside of our quantum bubble of space became compressed as the outward expanding force persisted to grow an equal and soon greater force began to resist, slowing the expansion till eventually it stopped and a rebounding effect of even greater force collapses it inward.

One concept that science has yet to grasp is that force itself is infinite, that light and energy may hold a density value that allows it to exist at a speed based on that density but that speed while considered constant depending on the environment in which it exists can be exceeded through the application of additional force.

THE SOURCE

The source is from this point as a whole, the entity we refer to as God, and in the moments after God's Birth is where we begin an understanding of why God is a part of all that exists. We are taught and learn about the concept of "The Big Bang" where force creates energy and that this energy expands to create what we refer to as space. We are taught this in school and through science and this is often where religion refuses science because most religions portray our creator as always has and will be.

This is only partially true, for using physics itself we gain a deeper understanding. It is true that after this point God is a part of all things, in every blade of grass, every rock, every form of life and the source of every atom itself, in every way, shape and form God does exist in literally every thing including in you, in every part of you. Often people refer to themselves and others as "God's Children". This is true, we are all and will forever be God's children even if we rebuke religion, deny God's existence entirely it matters not for that truth exists with and without your approval. God does not exist on prayers, nor is God petty enough to discard you simply because you lack the understanding. God's morality is God's own morality and in terms that can be understood easily it is refined to the utmost over such a vast amount of time it seems somewhat inconceivable.

Science states some 13.8 billion years have passed, this may be true but even if that is true that only defines our current existence. To make things simple let's consider 13.8 billion years of progression for which God can experience and learn, to think and to be. God now is and would be the most knowledgeable and understanding entity that will ever be, God would hold a morality and sanctity that includes not just one form of life but of all life. God would be from this point the creator of all things that we will ever know. The creator and we thus, the created. All life henceforth flows from the source itself, all the energy we use to think and feel to include our very souls themselves flow from the source.

All things shall and forevermore be part of the whole, the source we call God. Cosmic Alchemy exists. I refer to it as Spatial Equivalent Atomic Exchange (SEAE) and is used to represent the result of energy being converted into other forms. We see the basics of this when we look at the sun. The sun shines down and produces light; this light is absorbed by plants, and those plants convert that energy using photosynthesis to grow and reproduce. We also see another conversion from the sun where energy is released when light elements fuse into heavier elements. This process uses nuclear fusion of hydrogen into helium, helium into carbon and oxygen; oxygen into silicon, and silicon into iron.

Every particle that exists is converted and transferred in some way, shape or form into another. This can be detailed by referring to the circle of life. When we pass and are laid to rest in the earth, the particles that make up our body are then fertilizer for the plants and trees. Those trees pull in carbon dioxide and water and use the energy of the sun to convert this into chemical compounds like sugars that feed the tree. This chemical reaction creates oxygen, which is released by the tree, which we then breathe, our breath then creates carbon dioxide and the circle of life continues.

THE BEGINNING

The End has come and now it is time for The Beginning. This happens not only as defined by physics but also under the conditions of morality, compassion, true love, sanctity and sanctuary for this is when God awoke and realized what had occurred. In these moments however long or short it may have been, remember that the love that existed also became one and the greatest form of it took shape. God was overjoyed and also horrified at the reality of this event. Overjoyed to be and that while this did occur, the life that existed may have ended, but it also continued within Godself and that because for however long or short these moments may last, that everyone and everything of all that exists could too know the truth of existence not just as it was but what it would become.

In terms of simplicity, each life, each consciousness that was in existence is now within God and is now considered Godself, not extinguished as some may think but as one, saved in this sense. Though the physical body was no longer present the minds and consciousness of those who were remain. This leads to the creation of heaven or paradise, at least the first representation of it. The consciousness that was is now preserved eternally and essentially held in the hand of God henceforth.

As God began to be for the first time what I refer to as "the great pondering" has begun, considering how much knowledge was present and also considering that each mind would essentially be considered by present terms as a processor in a computer when God thought, it was using all knowledge and with the most powerful processor to ever exist. For simplicity's sake we can consider a comparison to our own brains where each mind within that collective consciousness was similar to a synapse. These synaptic responses occur much like ours do and if you consider it both like our own brains and with a capacity similar to a computer, the more active synaptic response and or processors, the greater the speed of thought and calculation is.

Here is where God unravels all that is and has ever been and begins to establish and solidify that which God is and is meant to be. It is also where we can establish a moment for which God begins to contemplate life, death, morality, sanctity, sanctuary and all the emotions and conditions that exist. This did not occur one by one, but rather all at once. This is why I refer to it as "the great pondering" for it is a pondering of such a magnitude in knowledge and information to identify it step by step in any simple way would take many lifetimes and also why it is "The Beginning".

Remember that all knowledge that existed now flows freely. That which was not known is now known and is not just known. It is understood in its entirety. This includes scientific knowledge and understanding of particles and far beyond. Religions that exist are also known and the connections between both are placed in the same container without prejudice and devoid of fault. As this collection of all life in existence now resides under one roof, creating what we consider "The Book of Life" which includes every form of life that ever was and is.

THE RETURN

After "The Great Pondering" a conclusion arises not just from the contemplation but also from the morality that now exists, a morality so complete and refined that it would be considered divine by any standard we could express. Such a morality is composed and created from all life and an understanding beyond just one form unfolds to encapsulate all that exists, giving way to a profound structure and depth of sanctity that it too, would be considered divine by any standard. So, with morality and sanctity God establishes the structure of sanctuary far beyond the terms of self.

God's thoughts turn from self and turn to selfless and as these concepts are grasped entirely, God comes to a decision, that decision is to return that which was taken away... Life, but with this decision, a truth is brought forth and that truth remains even still. In order for life to return to our existence as it was before, it must be done from scratch. Using the knowledge of all that exists, God sets in motion by will, the foundations to provide life anew.

The return of this energy back into existence so that life may grow once again would look quite similar to "The Big Bang." Creating an existence that can sustain and provide sanctuary to all life is, in my own eyes, complex but also quite simple. God of God's own free will gives up the body so that we may have the opportunity to be once more. So that we may once again learn to love life, we are granted this gift by the grace of God. So, too by the grace of God, will God hold our souls in God's hand and keep us safe from destruction as we establish our own soul's energy so it may exist eternally without God's hand to sustain its existence. So that one day, God can not only be the source of our existence but our friend and neighbor as an equal in which we exist side by side, not as one but as many. For this is the love of God.

I want to remind you this is just a basic understanding and that the further you break it all down and put it back together the more complete it becomes. I have left this in a simplistic form so that many may begin this process should they choose to. As you read through this book and grasp each concept both individually and as a whole your understanding will evolve with it until you obtain the truth for yourself. Each section may include parts of other sections, but it will begin to unravel the mysteries of our existence until you obtain absolute truth as God intended. Stand united under heaven so you may become your true self on earth as it is in heaven. God is not just beside you. God is inside you, as God is literally in all that exists.

In the next few sections, the specifics of who, what, when, where, why and how will be detailed and as you read and understand them, it may help to revisit these first three sections; as you do, you will discover for yourself the connections just as I did. Each pass will connect more and more of the world around you until you can put this down, walk out the door and see all the truths in existence for yourself. It may also help to read one section per day and ponder its truths for yourself.

Remember, all of this is "All For You".

PART 2:

The Basics...

How to connect to God

Now that we have more information on how God came to be, we can begin to apply a basic understanding through physics to understand this concept and how it is possible. To do this, we must take into consideration the fundamentals of several concepts. First is to understand that God holds a multitude of energy types at once, this means many emotional energies intermixed as one. So, this identifies that every emotional energy should be present in you, in order to connect.

We must also understand that in order to obtain that high emotional energy output, we must both activate multiple energies at once and retain enough of that energy in each of its forms, to reach this resonance state. The concept includes the understanding of sanctity and sanctuary, which is derived from the collective consciousness that makes the many different life forms within the collective itself. So, to simplify that structure and to best understand how this energy is formed at the source we turn to true love. True love is obtained by the collective consciousness through the knowledge of all life and the deep understanding that knowledge provides.

True love activates the most organic components and allows us to reach a peak resonance that can be obtained, and it is appropriate or at least acceptable to refer to these as emotional gates. This is where we activate our inner energy and maximize both our output and increase our internal capacity. Though this is not where it ends, we must also understand that when you take two forms of energy of the same type and place them together, they become indistinguishable and intermix to become one energy.

To detail this properly, we must think in terms of Energy and that God's energy resonates on a vibrational frequency that closely resembles true love. So, in order to connect to the source of that true love you must resonate under the same frequency. It is not magic, it is literal. One of the present functions we have that closely resembles it is "Wi-Fi". The closer you are to the frequency of true love the easier it is to connect. Energy of type "A" will not connect properly to energy of type "TL."

It helps to look at it like this: you are like a light bulb and the closer you get to resonating in terms of frequency to true love the easier it is for God to see you, if you imagine that every life form out there is also a light bulb and you look out across a sea of light bulbs and there is one bulb that shines brighter than the rest your eye would naturally notice it easier. The more energy of true love you hold, the easier you are to be seen and connect with. True love is literally the key here and this cannot be falsified. It must be as true as true can be. Something people tend to not realize is that true love is eternal. It transcends life and death and even transcends the physical and the spiritual. It is the most potent form of energy that creates and completes the soul itself as it so closely resonates with the creator itself. It is also the foundation for which heaven exists, and the reason in which you are capable of obtaining an eternal soul.

True Love generates all other forms of emotional energy all at once. It cannot even be explicitly defined even by God. If God was to define it, God would need to do so at such speed to God all progression would seem to stop entirely as God defines every expression, action, thought, and emotion in every way, shape, and form that has ever existed and when that is complete, the next moment begins and God would have to do it again for in each moment another concept of this love is created and this repeats eternally. If a human, or any life form for that matter, attempted to do this it would begin and never cease too for all eternity.

One of the only ways I could compare the sheer depth of it is to refer to it as the rain that falls from the sky; each drop of water that falls is in itself another expression of that love and as it lands upon the earth, it collects into the puddles, streams, rivers, lakes and continues till it gathers in such immensity that it forms the ocean itself, where it then begins to crash upon the shores of the heart. It continues as it evaporates into the sky and creates the clouds, which then falls again to create new forms of that love in an endless cycle of birth and rebirth.

Further, you must love this way, so truly and completely that all that you are flows forth to actually connect and communicate with the creator not just to be seen and heard but to hear as well. You must be this capable and hold enough true love's energy to do so. Consider it closely to this concept, if you were a very small battery, like a double AA and you connected that battery with an unrestricted flow to a nuclear reactor, it would melt that double AA battery destroying it. So God restricts and restrains this until such a time as the vessel is capable of doing so without being harmed. You must be capable of endless true love, a love so complete and true as true love can be. In this moment, you and God shall be of like mind, body, heart and soul, just as two separate energies of the same type intermix and become one, 120v appliance goes into a 120v plug, using a 220v charger causes damage.

I cannot stress the importance of understanding this concept as it literally leads you to heaven's gate, you must also realize that when you pass on, only the refined energy of your soul intermixes and regardless of how many emotions you're capable of using and holding in your mind at one time. You must grasp the reality that true love holds a unique energy. You cannot just activate every emotion and expect it to function. You must truly and completely love with all that you are so that you become as close to the same energy as God is.

Essentially, what you're attempting to do is connect to an entity of refined morality, sanctity, sanctuary, which is defined by trillions of different life forms and is composed of all the knowledge and understanding they hold and the emotional energy this generates. When you consider how many different life forms exist just on this one planet, and when including humans. You are talking about trying to resonate with all the emotional energy of every single one. The only way to do this, is to grasp that which is true love. True love is eternal, just being able to experience true love for even a moment is a miracle in and of itself.

True love is like sensory overload.

You try to feel it, your soul explodes.

It grows beyond what the flesh can hold.

You tap into the astral plane, and glide along heaven's lane.

Paradox of God's Existence

May God's Light find a way. Welcome to the Golden All Path.

One does not do good for God, one does because it is righteousness. One does not, for reward of salvation or even for immortality, one does not do, for eternity. One does because it comes from the soul. "To Be" your true self, seek no reward.

God does not weigh Godself to others. For God's morality is God's own as well. But it is by God's True Unconditional Love that we find the paths before us and the lessons to guide the people to Heaven the right way, as only you can forge your Eternal Soul, again remember who you are and let yourself become the greatest version of yourself that you can be, God awaits Humanity's Light.

Life is given to those so they may know Death.

Death is given to those so they may know Fear.

Fear is given to those so they may know Courage.

Courage is given to those so they may know Strength.

Strength is given to those so they may know Weakness.

Weakness is given to those so they may know Destruction.

Destruction is given to those so they may know Creation.

Creation is given to those so they may know Existence.

Existence is given to those so they may know Mortality.

Mortality is given to those so they may know Immorality.

Immorality is given to those so they may know Morality.

Morality is given to those so they may know Humanity.

Humanity is given to those so they may know Compassion.

Compassion is given to those so they may know Love.

Love is given to those so they may know True Unconditional Love.

True Unconditional Love is given to those so they may know God.

God is given to those so they may know Hope.

Hope is given to those so they may know Faith.

Faith is given to those so they may know Joy.

Joy is given to those so they may know Sorrow.

Sorrow is given to those so they may know Pain.

Pain is given to those so they may know Anger.

Anger is given to those so they may know Emotion.

Emotion is given to those so they may know Passion.

Passion is given to those so they may know Desire.

Desire is given to those so they may know Intention.

Intention is given to those so they may learn Truth.

The paradox is a means to understand parts of our existence and to identify it under a term of positive and negative where you move from one concept to another, you gather information and deepen your understanding as a whole until you arrive at a truth regardless of what that truth may be. You may find the paradox of God's existence I have created to be useful as is, but I would encourage you to create your own. It is best for an individual to learn by creating from scratch. Doing this gives you the best opportunity to solidify that knowledge and it is very important to be capable of doing so from nothing.

You may expand upon this also, but again, it is highly advised you begin from nothing, as this will present you with each piece one by one. You may find that the assembly of it changes depending on where you start. For instance, you may start at emotion, which if you notice is much further down the list than what I have. I encourage you to spend as much time as you need to do this. There is no wrong way to begin. You will eventually find yourself at the end, but to get to that end, you must begin.

The hope is that in doing so you become capable of not only identifying the source of something but refine yourself in the process. Self reflection is vital to understanding your own morality and once you understand your morality should you choose to do so you may refine it too. Processing the parts bit by bit using as much time as you need will assist you in removing or at least understanding who you are and who you choose to be.

For those that are interested, it may be time to consider taking into account your very thoughts themselves, for this too is fundamental in purifying and refining yourself, which is required and is best done in life rather than in death. Some folks do not choose to do this in life and find themselves doing so in the last moments of life, where they then hold vast amounts of regrets as they realize the immoralities they ignored or loved and cherished moments they squandered or lost. It can be beautiful to see a soul transform and transcend in this way, but it is even more beautiful to see it obtained before it's too late to enjoy life with that refinement.

The sooner this occurs, the better, not just for you but also for those you love. As your love is expressed and received more love is then returned. The more love you create and hold, the more energy your soul contains. Regardless of when this occurs for you specifically do not fret over seeing someone else do so while you have not. Each person has their own lessons, morals and loves to learn. Every individual will do so at their own pace. It is not a race by any means. But you must choose "to be" or "not to be" for that is the question only you can answer.

God may be all knowing but you are still capable of educating the creator using your choice. God may know the result of one answer and the other but you are still capable of free will and it is this free will that you use to choose.

Choose wisely...

What is a Pure Soul?

To understand this, it is best to use the term Refined as this is most accurate. A pure soul is a refined soul. The bio-energy that comprises your mind, as I call this Will, is the source of energy that creates your soul. Your soul is in a basic sense, fueled by the bio-energy produced, over time, as your mind de-fuses and re-fuses the synapse you identify as negative using the frontal lobe (cursing for instance) choices. Depending on your diligence over your thoughts and actions 24/7 you can refine your bio-energy and purify the mind, body, heart, and soul. Your soul cannot accept impure energy even when alive.

You cannot taint the soul and you certainly cannot trade, sell, give it away under any circumstances. If you produce immorality, it will not be accepted by your soul; it does not match the resonance and in life, it may seem like it doesn't matter. It truly does. You will have to face yourself, not your current self, which may hold many immoralities or petty concepts, but your true refined self. If you think your soul can't be angry at you. Think again; your soul is your refined self, just because it loves you doesn't mean it won't be angry. Anger created from love is quite strong, but take some solace to know your soul will understand that occurrence just as you do, if not more and will do so without hatred.

One of the hardest concepts for people to understand is that in order to be pure, you must purify your thoughts and actions. This can become difficult for some and most go through life with the idea that my thoughts are my own business. While this may be true in terms of legality and laws. It is not true in terms of the soul. To be a pure soul, you must produce pure energy, in thought, action and emotion. Do not confuse this for a reason to not protect yourself from others or to not protect your family or even an innocent. You have a right under God and Heaven to survive and protect the survival of others should it arise, but this does not mean you have any right to slaughter. Take serious heed here when I say you can not use this as a pretense to do harm. You cannot lie to your own soul or to God for that matter so don't even try.

When you bare yourself before the creator, you do this not in a sense of judgment, you do this to receive guidance and this occurs after you have been purified through the cosmic flow and arrive at the source. It is when all you are currently is presented and this means your morality, your loves, your joys, your sorrows and energy in its purest form is gazed upon by the creator. This is when God determines what is missing, by this, I mean if you lack an understanding in morality to fully grasp the sanctity of all life and the sanctuary for which it exists.

Your soul and its energy lay bare before the creator and if required you are then set upon the path to learn that which you do not know so that you may become your truest self, God is your guide to education and this education is given from scratch so that your very soul itself may be educated properly.

To lay yourself bare before the creator, is to present all that you are,
in mind, body, heart and soul.

What is Falling From Grace?

During your life, you begin to learn of Humanity and the Immoralities of Mortality with the Morality that created your Eternal Soul in Heaven, the energy produced by you during your life gets channeled and refined by your soul into its quantum structure, eternal spiritual energy occurs when you achieve enough energy that it gains enough electromagnetic tension that your energy cannot escape much like a black hole, the purest and most refined form of this energy comes from true love though falling from grace will happen as it occurs when said energy is depleted.

The reason your soul is then returned to life is so it may recharge and grow once more. Since your Inner Mind is Sensory based, you receive guidance through your own subconscious from this source, your own soul and in most cases, an external soul such as your ancestors, this occurs because the resonating frequency of like body is present, which allows them to also link with your Frontal Lobe through your subconscious, where you receive information often referred to as intuition. In truth, this is your mind being receptive to your own soul and to the Eternal Soul in Heaven as you exist here on Earth within the Mortal Body. This is "limited" and you cannot fall forever. Eventually, you will return but not as you intended, if you had desecrated the sanctity of a life so badly, God may require you to receive a lesson and as such, that lesson may include living as the life you so desecrated.

An example of this may be the slaughtering of an animal or performing some heinous act or acts during your life and never even taking the time to learn why this was an immorality. Before you can progress, you must learn the reasons for which your actions are wrong and as such you may not even return as a human but perhaps as a cow. So it is very important to reflect upon that which you do, to respect the life of all and to learn the morality of your immorality in life.

Know that it is God that defines this lesson. In most cases, it takes a very long time to regain the chance of Humanity. So do not disrespect it, honestly 2000 years is a long lesson, though it depends on how fast you learn your lesson that defines it. God's Love is unconditional but not weak. Trust me, being a plankton is disturbingly horrifying.

You do receive a defined grace from God, this grace establishes that God will preserve your soul until it becomes whole or complete. God's grace also is the reason the body was returned and a pathway to refinement is provided. In other words God is quite literally the most outrageous hero to ever exist. Just as we today refer to those that give the ultimate sacrifice in life to protect and save others as heroes. God is by far a hero to all that exists. For if God so chose to become whole again, all that is will no longer be. God does have free will, and I, for one, am thankful for that choice.

The grace of God refers to the conditions of the return and the prolonged salvation of your soul until it is complete. Though some do refer to the energy you produce to complete your soul as grace you created. Whatever you choose to call it, just remember that true love produces the most refined source. Those that obtain true love receive vast amounts of the purest of energy and more often than not, complete their soul sooner. There is no shortcut, and true love can not be falsified.

What is the difference between Eternal Spirit, Immortality, and God?

There is a difference between these structures, and while they are connected they remain separate nonetheless.

First: Eternal Spirit or Soul is what you become when you completely fill your soul's energy with true love or through true acts of kindness, which generates positive energy based on morality, sanctity and sanctuary and its density becomes great enough that it can maintain its existence without God's assistance through the energy some call Grace. If at any point in this process, you fall from grace and your energy is depleted, God then holds your soul and returns you to life so you may live, learn and grow "To Be" your true self on earth as it is in heaven. (True love, Morality, Sanctity and Sanctuary – consider these the pillars of your soul's creation.)

Second: Immortality is in essence, exactly what you think and refers to Immortality of the flesh, this does not mean you are indestructible. Immortality is to allow you the opportunity to continue to exist physically in the flesh once you have learned Sanctity of All Life and begin to refine your biological structure by slowly unlearning decay, as it stands, our bodies have incorporated particles within its base structures decay-able particles. In terms of religious concepts, this is when we refer to Adam and Eve, where we existed in paradise without decay and that decay was introduced by the consumption of the apple. When understanding this, it breaks down to detail that upon consuming the apple, regardless if it was through curiosity or through necessity, we introduce into our biological structure a decay-able particle. In one concept, it is understood that to grow and evolve, the body requires more energy and so this we identify as the necessity. When we reference it as a result of our curiosity, we still see the same result: we take a biological structure with non-decaying particles that are then provided with decay-able particles.

Consider it like this, if you are a creature that has never seen a banana and you consume it, while your body is capable of breaking down this structure, it has never seen something like potassium and identifies it as of like this structure and in nature it is found that biology tends to seek the greatest result with the least effort and it is much easier to use what already is then it is to create it from scratch. Though, in this case, the easiest is not best. Much like the panda's biology is designed to consume bamboo and convert it into the many structures it needs to exist. Potassium is a highly decay-able particle and while the biological structure is capable of breaking it down and using it, doing so introduces into what is considered a very durable structure a highly degradable particle. As this continues, the body replaces these non-decaying particles with the much easier to use decay-able particles.

Third: God is the collection of energy from the first collapse of existence that is now within what we would call a quantum bubble. As the space we know as existence collapses, this force moves faster than your body can even send signals to the brain, many times faster than it takes for nerves to send signals to the brain, coagulating the minds, and energy of all things relatively instantly. Creating the existence of God, which is created by life itself. This occurs because force is infinite.

What is Repentance?

Repentance is something you have to learn from within and it changes everything about your life as it changes your soul, this cannot be faked. Telling people to fear God is not only against God's will but is false teachings and will not create repentance as the people need to choose it of their own free will and this happens only after they learn of the reasons for which they commit immorality and why it is immoral, then choose to be greater then they were yesterday.

Through this, you become more "Noble " and earn Grace (refined energy) so that God can hold your soul in paradise if your energy is not enough to maintain itself already. Once you can maintain your soul yourself with your own energy, your soul is complete, you then become an Eternal Spirit with the Grace of God and should you choose to walk the Earth at will(return to life by choice). Until then, you are an incomplete soul, and without God's hand, you cannot exist in paradise because only purified or refined souls can be touched by God as God uses the energy we collected to do so. If you die without sufficient Grace or no Grace at all, you will recycle and do it again. If you recycle, you may not even be human upon your return to life.

You earn Grace through true acts of kindness, deep expressions of positive emotion and most notably, through true love itself, those acts that agree with your soul through morality, good will towards others and even the sanctity of all life. The key to this is to do and produce acts, thoughts and emotions that resonate with your soul. You must create and resonate with your true self, not your present self, unless, in some rare cases, you are already refined and have become your true self on earth.

Experiencing and being capable of true love, which I may remind you is eternal and endless in every way does more than just create energy, far more than that. In short the moments in which you hold true love. In those moments, God is looking at you with tears of joy, for you shine most bright. For God so loves those that love as God loves.

Know when you truly repent, you never commit that immorality again by choice, not because of fear for damnation but because of understanding and that many of these understandings are defined by sanctity and sanctuary of all life. You must learn morality and then commit to that morality with everything you are in mind, body, heart and soul. This is Repentance.

Your Repentance becomes you!

What is God's True Name?

God's name is unique for it contains every name known and not known, it is a string of all names combined into one as God is the collective of all life, God has "All Names" from "All" in "All Existence". To this end the "personal" name you choose to refer to God is not only correct but also incorrect or rather is just a part of it. God's name itself is a gift for which only God can give you. I do not use King, Lord or Jesus because God is not a landlord, nor does God desire any title and the use of God is God just as Jesus said so.

Consider also that because God is the source of all that exists and as such, resides within and throughout all things quite literally, so too is each thing that exists and its name a portion of God's true name. It is considerable to fully grasp the depths of this concept and when fully understood, it becomes clear that there is no wrong answer here. You may use any name you choose, for God is not petty. You may call to God however you choose for anything you choose within it resides at the source of God.

When you love thy neighbor, you too love God. When you love thy spouse, you too love God. When you love the grass, the birds, the bees, you too love God. Within all that exists resides the energy of the creator, the source itself is God. Some things may contain greater amounts of that energy. They may be bigger or smaller, but regardless of size, there is still no wrong answer. What God seeks is not your obedience or fear but your love in its truest form possible. God seeks true love.

To identify God's True name in mortal tongue would require several things, one is the gift of Ludwig van Beethoven, next you would need to be an Empathic person of considerable ability, then you would need a photographic memory which includes emotion. The translation would begin with the Empathic transfer into memory through emotion, this emotion would be converted into sounds and vibrations using the Gift of Beethoven. Only an individual capable of fully grasping and feeling the sound through the cosmic vibrations can unwind the string of names correctly enough to repeat the name of God. This, of course, would continue endlessly as you attempt to recite the names of all things in one continuous stream of words.

In present terms, it would be considered more like an energy you feel, this energy would be the truest and most complete form of love that exists. In simple terms, God is not Human and as such does not use Words as we do. The spoken language is a construct created by the creation, not the creator. All structures therein are just interpretations, though some may be more accurate than others. Understand that when words are used it is Human and not God.

For God shall speak not with the words of man but to the heart and soul itself.

What is God's Family?

We are all God's family, within us all is as within all things organic or inorganic, resides from the source of God's energy it remains true that all that is are fundamentally part of God and that all life and all things are, therefore also both part of God and are God's family, this includes even rocks. God's family is everything and everywhere. You may refer to it in the same terms as you would Godself. Cherish and love all that is and has been, for within it resides the creator as both the created and as God.

It is very important to understand that you are God's family and that to sit at the table of God is only possible when you are of like mind, body, heart and soul. This means you will resonate under the same frequency as God does until it is almost as if you are one. Essentially, the greater the resonance, the greater the connection. When considering this, it may become difficult to maintain the concept of self at times. For some, this can be confusing and when viewed by others, appear as if you have lost your mind. But in truth, it is simply that you are aligning yourself to an extent that you are of like, mind, body, heart and soul to that of the creator.

When some experience this, they tend to be unable to isolate or differentiate between it. This is not a bad thing nor is it immoral but it must be understood that you are still you. Your soul may be derived from the source and resonate with the energy of the creator, but you are still one soul, whereas God is the collection of all. This is not a means to say "I am God incarnate." Though you may hold within you God's energy and resonate greatly with that energy, it is still improper to do so. God is Godself and if you truly did resonate to such an extent you become one with God, the morality of God would also flow forth. In either case, you would not only know that you are not God incarnate but just a portion of Godself as you have and were before, that is currently resonating greatly, as you are aligning yourself to the energy that is true love, which is of like mind, body, heart and soul of God.

Resonating in this way is possible and usually only occurs for a moment, it is quite intense and generally lasts for a very short time. In this resonance, you connect to the source and elevation of your mind begins to grant clarity. This clarity provides a deep understanding and even absolute truth, which is devoid of self desire, of self gain and is pure in every sense of the word, it is where you experience divinity but know this state as all states of the mind are is very difficult to maintain and it is also true that all mental states change. This comes from mental fatigue and becomes clearer the longer you attempt to maintain this state of existence.

As God is the bio-energy created from all living creatures of the last existence combined with all the energy from all things, God is also all current life, past and present and will include all future life as well. It is because of this that God looks upon all as family. To God we are, as all life is "God's children", God's Family. God has no problem walking beside you as an equal, below you as a barrier, and above you as True Unconditional Love. Peace on Earth to all under Heaven and above for it is between this that Humanity resides, grows and blossoms into the greatest Kingdom the Cosmos will ever know, Humanity shall give birth to itself and creation under God Indivisible with justice under Heaven and sanctity and sanctuary to all that exist.

Where is Heaven?

Heaven can be considered to some as where we go when we move on from the physical into the spiritual, and in some ways this is true, nothing wrong with that. But Heaven does have a physical location. To some people, it is paradise and there is nothing wrong with that either; to others, they consider Heaven to be God's hand and some consider God's hand to be paradise. Nothing wrong with either of those things, for what you consider paradise or heaven is yours to choose.

In this sense, understand that within this existence there is a location that is physical in which God resides and also where Eternal souls gather. God's location resides at the very source of energy in which all energy flows. To find God physically, you follow the cosmic flow of energy to the source itself. This collection of energy is where those unable to maintain their own souls reside until it is time to return to life.

What I consider to be paradise is, wherever my true love is standing. Besides my true love is my paradise, but there is a place in existence which some would consider to be paradise which exists. This is where souls gather, who have obtained the ability to exist without the assistance of God's hand which are capable of maintaining self as they have completed or gathered enough of their own energy within the soul to do so.

While some would not call such a place paradise, some may and as such, I will refer to this as the location of paradise. Your paradise may be different and that is ok, but this gathering of the eternal souls would also be located by following the natural cosmic flow of existence. Some have referred to this place, to heaven and to God in the past as Sirius.

Know that regardless of where it is now at this very moment, it too must follow the basics of physics and the concept to understand is SEAE or cosmic alchemy; this is to mean that should Sirius cease to be, that just means its location is changing. It is not required for it to be in one spot and while we may only know of it during our life as at this location. It will not mean that should that location or star, planet, collection of energy disperse in any way, that it is gone. It will simply gather and exist in its next natural place as it is meant to be. While it may reside at this physical location now it may reside at a different one in two billion years from now.

For instance, should it be identified that Sirius is the location of either heaven or paradise and disaster befalls this location and it, as a result, no longer exists, the energy is not and that energy will simply flow to the next natural location. The greatest collection of energy, or rather the source of "The Big Bang" is where God resides and would be identified also by its resonating frequency. Though, understand that what you consider heaven, paradise or otherwise, is yours to define just as I have defined that my heaven, my paradise is at the side of my true love.

Open your heart and your mind will follow.

What is Baptism?

Currently, Baptism is regarded as ceremonial in nature, which is meant to be a public display of your acceptance of the practice where you symbolically wash away your immoralities and begin anew. Immersing in water is the physical act which is used to represent this and not only meant for you but also for the community in which you reside. By doing so you publicly declare to be a follower of that practice and the commitment and faith therein.

Far be it for me to say otherwise, but please understand baptism is a method of purifying that you yourself must employ to cleanse the mind, body, heart and soul of immoralities brought forth by your mortal self using bathing in water to symbolize the washing of physical dirt and symbolically the immorality of the mind. It does not end there, however, since the general concept of baptism is to cleanse and wash thyself clean you can and should perform this everyday and in as many ways as possible to include the drinking of life giving water. Fasting is another form of cleansing and this helps to remove toxins that build up from the food and water you consume. Drinking water does contain toxins like fluoride, which is a neurotoxin and unwanted heavy metals such as lead, it is important to consume filtered or purified water to maximize the benefits you receive.

While it is good to understand its current uses, it is important to also understand that while some practices state it must be done by someone of authority, understand that in terms of your own soul, you are the most authoritative and that you yourself must of your own free will choose to cleanse and discard thoughts and actions that are immoral. Understanding why those thoughts and actions are immoral and how you can discontinue them is important.

I use a prayer "I drink the tears of Joy so I may know Sorrow.", I then drink a sip of water. I then say "I drink the tears of Sorrow so I may know Joy.", I then take another sip of water. This may be spoken aloud or in private. It is a Frontal Lobe choice to cleanse thyself. It also cleanses the internal body of toxins, which in turn helps elongate life using biologics as the guide. Every day, God chooses education over destruction, as should you.

It is also advised to show respect for the food you eat, to the life you consume to continue to exist. In this way, you may pray and give thanks; some practices do this quite often and it is encouraged to do this before you consume anything. In this way, you can show your commitment to yourself and to the life you consume. At first, you may find it difficult to remember that before you drink water or take a bite of food to pray and give thanks, but with a bit of diligence, you will become more accustomed to doing so and it will be easier to remember over time. If you forget, simply pause and remind yourself to do so; ensure that at this time, you then do it and apologize for your forgetfulness.

Praying while you bathe is also helpful, the more you commit, the greater the result, but if you find yourself overwhelmed by doing so, relax. The prayers don't need to be extensive and complicated, since sincerity is what is important. The greater your sincerity the better, even if all you do is "Thank you", if it is said with extreme sincerity it shall be far greater than a five minute prayer without any sincerity. Quality not quantity is key.

Why Immorality and not Evil or Sin?

Immorality is a much more appropriate term, as it removes many misconceptions while providing accuracy to the source itself. The root of your immorality often resides with ignorance; while some may consider this word to be insulting, that is not true, it is the acknowledgment of not knowing. Using the term immorality, we can identify that what has occurred is immoral and, in doing so, begin to educate ourselves on the morality that is not present.

It is important to understand also that the negative is simply the absence of positive. Some would argue that evil is to refer to the commission of bad deeds. In truth, the commission of a bad deed is the absence of the knowledge and understanding of why and what makes it so. This occurs because you are ignorant of the morality therein and if you were on the receiving end, you would not approve of such a thing. Immorality, when used properly, identifies that a morality is missing and provides a stepping stone to that understanding. This does not mean you cannot do so of your free will.

It is also important to understand that bad deeds occur often because the one performing them lacks one of the most important truths that exists, which is true love. A vast majority of the immoralities exist because true love is absent and conditions of self desire are present. Self desire promotes the taking for self gain, which leads to someone being taken from often needlessly. When you take far more than you need from someone, it may cause harm in some way, shape or form. When you ignore morality through ignorance, you perform an immorality.

Sin is improper and implies an unlearnable morality, that even if you at the very core of who and what you are, even through ignorance, do something that you could never recover and that defies God's will itself. While some lessons given may be harsh and some might consider them to be a form of damnation, this is just not true. Understanding repentance will help you grasp the reality of this, but repentance is not meager and when you become educated in immorality and become repentant, it changes everything quite literally.

The terms used as Evil or Sin, or even Satan, confuse the mind from understanding true unconditional love by guiding the mind into the idea God could, would, or should eternally destroy one's children or creations. Though life and death within existence are presently undeniable truths, we cannot ignore or escape them. It is but a lesson upon which we continue till we become the existence that is our creation of Eternal Life and the Eternal Soul naturally the right way, from scratch... This fear of death is real and true. But from it, we find courage, and through courage, we find True Strength. This strength God cherishes and loves within you all. But to call God's Family, Pet, Plant, Creation, by something which portrays hatred... is a disrespect that Humanity must accept and stop. Become God's family and "join Humanity".

True Strength comes from within.

True strength is born from love, the truest love that exists would create the truest strength to exist.

True love exists for it is within me.

<u>Why is the Loss of Life Tragedy?</u>

First we must understand that when life is gone, the soul loses the ability to generate energy gained from existing as living. Though by God's grace, we shall exist in heaven, it is only by God's grace that those who have not obtained the ability to exist without God's hand that we may obtain the opportunity to do so ourselves.

There are also those we leave behind: our loved ones, our children and our friends; the amount of this loss is endless. So many moments of laughter, of joy and love are no longer present. Other joys exist, but those specific moments and the unique things in which it holds are not.

With that said, there is another reason the loss of life is tragic. So tragic, in fact many would consider it the source of immorality in such things as suicide or murder, aka slaughter.

Within each person there exists an intelligence; this intelligence in itself is unique. Each mind has the ability to generate things such as art, music, science, philosophy and religious contexts. These unique things are born when an individual obtains an understanding of their true self.

Take, for instance, an individual with the ability to create music from nothing without even being able to hear. Such as Beethoven, had this life been extinguished before the reality of his existence was made clear, the works he created known. All the wonders and joys he would or could have created would be lost.

Where would it have left us?

How many other creations would not exist?

How many untold joys lost?

How much love that would have been is gone?

Each and every single person has a gift of humanity that resides within their heart and soul. Life allows us to draw it out from the depths and form it so that others may know it exists. When a life is gone, that possibility is gone with it. That creation now remains untold and the world may never know the truth of its existence. Some of these creations allow and give others the ability to generate love; without that piece some may not acquire it, may not experience it. The loss of that love, that joy from our existence is in itself a tragedy.

Another individual may have been capable of creating a composition, this is true, but that unique piece, the forms it holds would be lost. In this way the loss of even a single life is a tragedy upon humanity itself. With each loss of life another priceless gift is too lost.

These gifts can be even so great that they alter our world forever, cures for cancer, cures for diseases, infinite energy, interstellar travel, quantum relativity, marvels to behold in all shapes, all conditions, and within each and every single one of us this truth exists. From a single song, a form of creation in any way exists as an untold treasure that could unfold, allowing that person to transcend that which they are and become that which they are meant to be, their true self.

Consider what would have happened had the life of Jesus been ended at birth...

This is the reason such things are a tragedy, be it for any reason such a loss may be so great from a single life, a single soul that departs, it could alter and change every life henceforth for the rest of eternity.

These gifts are more valuable than you can imagine, gifts we must nurture and cherish always and with it, the life for which makes it possible. Not just the life you have but the lives of others, for in them and you exists that very truth.

Nourish and cherish the life you have and the lives of others, respect the gift of our sanctuary and the sanctity of all that exists; this includes all life. While elephants may not speak our specific language but if we taught them mathematics they would make every PhD on the planet appear as a child.

Intelligence is not just human. It exists in all things big and small. In different ways, for different reasons. Just because that life has no interest in music or science does not mean they have no worth or hold no form of intelligence.

Take a moment and try to answer these questions.

Have you ever contemplated what it means to the grass when you step in it?

Have you ever regretted stepping upon an ant?

Do you ask forgiveness for the microbes that die when washing your hands?

Answering these questions can assist you in understanding the life that exists all around you in every moment of every day.

Have you ever thought about the fact that rice balls are made of rice babies?

Dedicated to all those who have departed and that will depart for all eternity.
Cherished is the gift of life.

Sanctity of life or Sanctity of Human Life?

How can we properly define Sanctity of Life?

To do this, we will begin by defining each word itself as we break down what it means:

Define Life:

1. The condition that distinguishes animals and plants from inorganic matter, including the capacity for growth, reproduction, functional activity, and continual change preceding death.

In a Sentence: "Both science and religion seek to understand the source of life itself."

Define Sanctity:

1. The state or quality of being holy, sacred, or saintly. Ultimate importance and inviolability. In a Sentence: "The site of the tomb was a place of sanctity for the ancient Egyptians."

Define sanctity of life:

1. The term sanctity of life means the extent to which all life is considered precious. In a Sentence: "Respect the sanctity of all life within existence for it is a sacred place."

Define sanctity of human life:

1. The phrase sanctity of human life refers to the idea that human life is sacred, holy, and precious.

In a Sentence: "Often confused with survival, the human species considers the sanctity of human life over the sanctity of all other life."

Let's Recap, try answering in your own words the following #1-6 then read the answers:

1. Define life.

2. Define sanctity.

3. Define sanctity of life.

4. Define Sanctity of Human Life.

5. Which one does the Bible teach?

The Bible is currently teaching: Sanctity of Human Life.

6. Which one would God teach?

God teaches Sanctity of Life, "All Life".

God knows that we all will have moments when we realize things we thought were, "ok" are "not". It is normal and natural to gain information and to grasp a concept that is painful to understand. We all will have this moment when we begin to truly understand who we are and what we are doing. That pain will help you understand the morality from the immorality you had been ignoring. This process will repeat until your immorality is gone and just morality remains. This is the Refinement or Pure Soul I spoke about. Over time and with sincerity, you will connect with your Eternal Soul and with a bit of diligence in thoughtfulness and self reflection. You will solidify your morality and become your Eternal Self on Earth as it is in Heaven.

Understanding Immortality

Learning about Immortality and Sanctity of All Life is about understanding; through this understanding, we can identify the means in which we find true peace, within ourselves through the love of life to all. We can accept now and understand the exact methods used to create life to include God's Birth.

Many things in today are used to point out and do harm, this is not a competition. God does not exist on prayers or the souls of others. God does not require your energy to exist at all. God is created from life itself. From the void, we exist naturally, just as God does. God is not condemning you or anything else. Life exists and this existence was made from scratch. The purpose of using our minds is to direct our choices and this will allow us to refine ourselves just as the creatures of nature do. Using a specific protein that can be manipulated and flavored in any way, we want to include textures, densities and with this replication, we can easily move from animal products while being 100% green to include the energy that it takes to produce these products.

We can obtain self-sufficiency in this protein over many generations of refinement; our own biological structures will then become selective in isolating this protein. When this happens, we will begin to develop increased productivity when breaking down the protein, which leads also to the body developing a specific way to convert these basic proteins into everything our bodies need; this will become what I call protein overgrowth. Through this, we can become much more than we are today.

Immortality itself through natural biological evolution is already shown and proven through the animal kingdom. As we go from photosynthesis to the immortal jellyfish, each branch adapts to its specific repetitive input into the body. To ignore this is not science. What we need to do is conduct ourselves in the same way and choose the correct protein, minerals and vitamins we need. Then isolate them and produce vegan products with these specific properties so our biology can begin to learn through a consistent and repetitive input as it is meant to. The more we flood our bodies with massive varieties of different things we reset our progression or rather confuse our biology. We are going nowhere in terms of evolutionary progression towards immortality of the flesh; the panda is further along than we are.

Through science, Humanity can erase the immorality that exists and was required to create life from scratch. Life has already shown us millions of miracles, and this is how it is obtained. As a species, we must choose, and for the future, of all. We must choose right.

Immortality of the flesh is possible but is only obtained through biology using the sanctity of all life. As we progress as a society, we grant more sanctity to other creatures that we exist beside. This must be done from scratch so our biology can unlearn decay. This occurs as we continue to grant more sanctity and sanctuary to other creatures. The progression of society's morality identifies this as we identify animals such as horses or endangered species; we protect them. Giving them sanctity and sanctuary, laws are created to prevent them from being consumed or destroyed.

God does not make sippy cups.

The Holy Grail

The Holy Grail is often revered for its mysticism and mythical lore as a blessed chalice or bejeweled grail that could offer its gift of immortality to those that drink from it. While this may be represented in certain religions and even considered the ultimate holy relic, let's take a look at what science can define about this concept.

In science, we take notice of several structures that could lead to proper identification of this concept. Those structures are biology, sanctity, sanctuary and social compassion. So let's take a look at biology and what we can establish to give us a better understanding of this concept of immortality.

In biology, we identify a specific type of animal. This animal is called the immortal jellyfish, the scientific name for this animal is Turritopsis Dohrnii. This animal has the potential to live indefinitely and according to science, there may be jellyfish that live today that even lived 66 million years ago. This jellyfish has a unique ability and can be active when injured or when starved; when food sources become so scarce it cannot maintain its adult form, its biology activates a reversion process where it reverts to an infant stage called the polyp stage. Effectively maintaining its lifecycle potentially forever, however, this does not mean they are indestructible.

Science has yet to fully study these animals entirely but this is a miraculous biological marvel itself. So here we see an identified scientific biological structure capable of providing a form of immortality, this unique biological adaptation is brought on through a repetitive need defined by the cellular structure in a harsh and unforgiving environment.

Another animal we look at is the panda. Pandas have a very interesting biology as well. While they are fluffy and adorable to most, there is a very unique adaptation they too have obtained. This however is where we will focus our attention because they more closely resemble our base biological structure. These creatures have through many generations adapted to survive eating primarily bamboo.

These animals have adapted to this because they were most likely forced to, as most adaptations in biology are not a choice and tend to occur because of need or random mutation. When these changes occur and they persist to enhance the basic survivability of the animal, it eventually spreads or overtakes its competitors. The panda's body has adapted to be able to extract and convert a vast majority of what it needs from just bamboo. Their diets consist primarily of this and have become enhanced through this repetitive input, highly proficient at doing so compared to other creatures like humans.

So, over vast generations of forced input and the increasing need for survival these adaptations occur naturally and provide these animals a much needed advantage to maintain its continued existence. Without these harsh conditions these adaptations may not even occur because the many generations would have input different materials and the biology may not have activated.

So we now understand that biology, through repetitive inputs, typically brought on by harsh conditions and the intense need for continued survival, can and have activated enhanced productivity of selected food sources and reversion of cellular growth itself. So, The panda helps us identify that biology can direct and enhance our productivity based on consumed particle intake and the immortal jellyfish identifies that starvation itself can even initiate cellular changes as intense as reversion in age.

So, let's take a look at how sanctity plays a part in this concept. As we all know currently, we need to be the panda so to speak. We need to educate our biology to accept and adapt to create advanced protein development. This is important because we must begin to intensify the repetitive inputs of the basic concepts to initiate an enhanced productivity in the materials we consume. This happens by providing sanctity to more and more animals. Currently, we consume whatever we want and have a very diverse food source. One key aspect to activate adaptation is to repeatedly input the same sources into the biological structure. Over generations, this will produce as a positive interaction, the desired enhancement. Our stomachs will become more proficient at breaking down those specific inputs, and our bodies will eventually be able to convert from those inputs any additional particles the body may need.

This blends into sanctuary as we begin to provide sanctity; we then also provide sanctuary to those animals, as we know there is an encroaching human development into the natural habitats of present wildlife, as we encroach upon and remove the natural habitats of many of the animals present today these animals begin to dwindle. When they dwindle so much, they get placed on an endangered species list; when this happens, laws that we established place upon those animals a protected sanctity of their life and right to exist. We then establish some form of sanctuary for them to exist so that they may have a proper natural home to live in. Sanctity and sanctuary tend to go hand in hand and this is most notable from wildlife reserves such as Yellowstone National Park, where we have many species and the entire area is protected quite vigorously.

We had hunted the Buffalo almost to extinction, quite literally, they were our food, clothes and livelihoods and were killed to such an extent it was easily considered mass slaughter. Had we completely wiped them out, it would have been called genocide. So today, we provide them with a stable and well protected expanse of land in which they presently reside and flourish. This is just one example, and many other species are protected all over the world now.

As we continue to provide these animals more and more protections, as they continue to enter the endangered species lists, we then activate a protection and provide them, in most cases a sanctuary. Sanctity and sanctuary are also provided in other ways to animals, such as dogs and cats. We now have animal rights laws that provide dogs and cats a basic right to exist and prevent them from being needlessly harmed or abused and even neglected. When you have these companions, you are obligated to care for them. Provide them food and water, even proper housing and basic comforts. In this way, we continue to provide more and more protection to animals.

The horse, for instance, is nearly considered to have the same rights as a human does, in some cases more rights. This is referred to as social compassion and is one of the many ways we become greater as a species as we provide more sanctities and sanctuaries not just to ourselves but to other creatures. We began by providing other humans sanctities, then we began to pass those sanctities to animals. This presents us with our next concept in obtaining immortality.

With every sanctity we provide, we remove an animal, creature or other lifeform from the list of consumption. As we narrow down that list of acceptable consumable foods, we begin to isolate specific types of food that are allowed to be eaten regularly. Establishing a specific structure for which we permit on a regular basis to be used by our own biological structures. This isolates and promotes adaptations over many generations. It may take a long time to reach this point, but eventually, we will create and maintain a stable diet quite simply because we choose to.

From diverse consumption to specific consumption to isolated consumption we provide biology the opportunity to become like the panda. But this is not where we end our discovery of what science can detail about this process. The key to human immortality exists in the unlearning of decay. We evolved from an organism that had no decay; we also didn't do much of anything really and in order for biology to grow and evolve into what we are today, it consumed other materials. During this consumption, we gained greater amounts of energy, spurring on our adaptive and evolutionary growth into the diversity of life that exists all over the planet.

So, we look back to a religious construct referred to as Adam and Eve and the Garden of Eden. In this stage, we would consider the structure of the body to be without decay. The cells that made our genetic structures had highly durable materials constructed the hard way from scratch. When we consider the information that we hear in many religious practices today, they speak of the eating of the apple. Which casts us out of paradise for an immorality commonly considered desire, temptation, even curiosity. So what happens to a biological construct composed of highly durable and maintainable structures when it eats a banana or apple?

The answer might surprise you, biology tends to go for the highest gain at the lowest effort. This is predominant in nature in many ways and while our bodies are capable of digesting an apple or a banana, it doesn't mean we should. These fruits contain a material considered one of the most decayable particles known… Potassium. So our bodies that had never before consumed something like Potassium and had up to this point only created what it needed the hard way which ensured its most effective and durable structure is now looking at this particle and that this particle is very similar to this other particle it creates. So it takes the highest gain and easier to use route and moves that particle to replace or to build a cell in the body. As time goes on, this continues, and bit by bit, those previously highly durable and made from scratch materials that comprised your entire body are replaced with highly decayable and easier to obtain particles.

When you look at this in a religious concept as the banishing from the Garden of Eden by the eating of the apple and refer to the Garden of Eden by the perfect and complete body with the most durable structures in our biology and the banishing in reference to learning of decay through the placement of highly decayable particles, you begin to understand how this concept is directly reflected into and expressed by science. So, to obtain and become as we once were, the non decayable biological structure, we must teach our biology to unlearn decay. To do that we must isolate and repeatedly input the same food sources rather than a highly diverse source to initiate adaptation and to literally enforce the biological structures to discontinue the use of decayable particles as a base for the construction of new cells.

This is how we become immortal in the flesh naturally from scratch through biological evolution using the sanctity of all life. Our own society itself will, over time, naturally move towards this but it won't hurt to start now.

Basic stages of sanctity:

Sanctity of human life	- Stage 1
Sanctity of animal life	- Stage 2
Sanctity of plant life	- Stage 3
Sanctity of microbial life	- Stage 4

God does not hand immortality to those who do not adhere to the sanctity of all life.

To do so would mean you would devour all life forever.

Survival not Slaughter

It is important to know that slaughter is not moral and by no means permitted under heaven as a means to exist. Some may not understand the difference between these two concepts clearly. One defines why animals exist and enter heaven when they pass on. This is because they follow the terms of survival. God's morality identifies that you have the right, even under heaven to survive.

This, however, does not mean you have the right to slaughter; under terms of slaughter, you kill needlessly and not for survival. Animals do not have grocery stores, or farmers markets for which they may obtain food. They exist without this and thus enter into a condition identified as survival. To this extent, the lions, however gruesome it may seem, when they hunt an animal and eat it, they have to. It is a requirement for them to survive to exist, for without it, they would otherwise perish.

That same term is applied to you, while the consumption of other life currently is required, the consumption of animal life is not. You can live a very healthy and productive life without the use of slaughter to exist. Regardless of what people say today, it is no longer a required concept for a vast majority of us to kill animals to live. This is an immorality that the world as a whole needs to understand: your life is no more important than any other life. This includes the ants you step on as you walk around. Most ignore this act and attempt to justify it in some way. Genocidal slavery is slaughter and is currently being conducted quite literally just to please your taste buds. This is a desecration of the sanctity of all life and quite a heinous one.

God grants us this sanctity and the opportunity to create and protect the sanctuary of all. While society depicts a mediocre adherence to such sanctity and sanctuary it does not actually adhere to it. Within the structures of today's world, sanctity is only given to some. The result is clearly false sanctity with the condition that sanctity be granted to some, provided humans are in control. That sanctuary should be given as long as it is not stopping or slowing down the economic activity of humans and thus, we continue to destroy and make excuses to do so every single day.

We use terms such as "I need" when it is actually "I want". We create destruction under the guise of our own prosperity without giving other lives that same opportunity as we force them into cages, smaller habitats and even commit other species to be subjects of genocidal slavery as we slaughter them, just to please our taste buds.

We use distorted versions of God's will to protect ourselves and create slaughter under this distorted image. We give ourselves the idea that we are some kind of supreme being in which God is permitting the slaughter of life to feed either someone's bank account or to provide you with a tasty morsel.

These are desire based concepts and should be discarded. There is a huge difference between slaughter and survival. It is to our benefit that we learn this difference as soon as possible. If a parent found their child devouring all their other children because they found them tasty, what do you suppose that parent would say?

Would it be a pleasant conversation?

The Vows of True Love

Today we have controversy with the way vows of love and marriage are performed.

These vows violate that which is true love. For this fact remains true beyond all others. True love is eternal.

During the marriage vows, which present-day churches use and in many other ceremonies, the term "till death do you part" exists and this itself is a violation of true love.

As I explained, true love is eternal and as such, it transcends life and death, time and space; it is a force for which heaven was crafted and the very source of our soul's eternity. Our souls are crafted from the source and as such, this source is made by the energy of true love in all life.

By being forged from the source which is made by this true love, it is imperative to understand that true love is the source of energy for which your very souls are capable of eternal life beyond death.

It is also granted by the grace of God and this grace is given from the source. That source is energy made from true love. For God to grant this to you and preserve your soul in heaven until you yourself have obtained that energy to exist without God's hand, you must grow in energy; the most prominent method is to obtain true love. When this occurs you will become your true self on earth as it is in heaven.

When you obtain this energy yourself, God's hand is no longer required to hold your soul for you to exist and when this occurs, you may walk this earth at will. This means you may return to life when you choose to or exist in spirit for as long as you choose. For in this state, with this energy, your soul has enough density to return its expended energy back into itself. When you obtain this energy but have not learned the sanctity of all life, you still do not expend energy during your education in the here-after and so are not recycled. You may be required to learn the lessons from God, but if those lessons can be obtained through a means without having to return to life it shall be so, this condition will be between you and God.

With this in mind it is a good idea to discard these words in your vow of love under heaven and retain a vow of true love as your love is eternal. If it is not eternal, then it is not true love.

To every pastor or ceremonial conductor on the planet, I encourage you to stop claiming death can separate the love of the soul from its soulmate.

True love is Eternal.

How can I purify my Mind?

You do this through purification of thought. When you want to control yourself in thought and as the brain likes to do, it attempts to automate signals to the frontal lobe; this can be controlled and reprogrammed using choice. Here is how this works.

The system organizes the signals and attempts to direct them from the subconscious to the frontal lobe. During this process, we get seemingly instant access to these thoughts. This was designed and influenced by survival. When you see a bunch of leaves in the bush, your brain automatically attempts to show you a face. The same is said for hearing; when you're around certain noises like a fan it will attempt to organize it into a related signal to determine a voice or word. These signals originate from survival instincts and automated systems to support it. As we attempt to reprogram this we must do so through diligence and sincerity. Diligence gives us repetition and sincerity gives us the charge which is received by the synapse it passes over during the thought, which in turn increases the residual energy it gains from each signal.

To complete this properly, we must interrupt that signal and, using our choices, educate ourselves on how we want our subconscious to react or respond to these inputs. These inputs can come from anything in our body and often are misunderstood. The use of your frontal-lobe to enforce your will of choice over this response is key to discharging the unwanted synapses energy and directing the charge toward the choice or desired response, such as sexuality. When you have a thought of sexuality and you may even receive images or physical inputs such as being aroused, you must interrupt this signal. I do this by refusing it. Even saying directly, even in thought "no" or "stop it" and redirecting it to something else like a moral or positive thought. What kind of moral or positive thought depends on you and your choice.

Understand that biology in most cases, is automatically sending signals based on stimuli; sexuality is not love. It is a function of biology created from evolution promoting reproduction to increase the chances of survival.

You see this process with human calculators as they have programmed their brains to return digits. Whereas I have done so to return true or false, I do this because it is more inclusive and when I am missing information, I can then re-evaluate the information and work through any segments not true. Through diligence and sincerity, you may progress fast or slow. This I refer to as mental-elevation.

Now, in today's world mental elevation might classify me as a superhuman but in reality these things are learnable and in no way make me superior under any circumstance as it's no different than one person knowing how to swim and another person not. For this purpose the Paradox of God's existence may be applied. Mental elevation is a process of generating energy in thought to enhance it.

"The gift of mental power comes from God, Divine Being, and if we concentrate our minds on that truth, we become in tune with this great power. My Mother had taught me to seek all truth in the Bible." - Nikola Tesla

What is Mental Elevation?

Your brain is a particle generator; as you think and remain in refractive thought, your synapses absorb energy while remaining in refractive logical processive thought. You create a cyclic motion in which the energy travels and you unlock those synapses each time the thought refracts. This process unlocks the synapses over time and provides advanced cognitive thought. While in refractive thought, the synapse stores residual energy and produces advanced cognitive abilities. Each particle of energy that passes over a synapse leaves behind a trace amount of energy like in batteries; it retains more energy and this energy produces clarity and permits the thought to become enhanced by each refraction. Eventually, you not only produce advanced cognitive thoughts but generate enough energy to connect to the subconscious and as human calculators do receive responses as the signal carries with it enough energy to return. You can even determine what responses you receive from the subconscious.

Understanding how to utilize this is important as with its use the mind becomes elevated in thought. Extensive use of this refractive logical processive thought creates elevation in your mind, be aware that it can become fatigued and as all mental states are they must at some point change. This will be referred to as Mental Fatigue, when this fatigue sets in simply rest.

In order to produce high energy values in the synapses, you utilize mental elevation. This becomes a learned tool and while some may consider its use to be superhuman it is actually a learned ability that everyone is capable of even animals. As stated previously it is no different than one individual knowing how to swim and another not. As you do so it is also important to understand how to do this properly as with most conditions it is important to use refractive thought properly.

Elevating the mind naturally and properly begins by assigning specific functions and methods to the thought process itself to form logical processive thoughts to ensure it maintains a structure that the mind becomes accustomed to using over and over again and eventually without even trying. It begins with verifying the thought through each function to obtain a purified or refined thought. The steps are important and this is to ensure that the energy itself is refined and pure as it includes emotional energy. Negative energy often dilutes the thought itself and produces falsified information based on self or, rather, what you want instead of what actually is. When using this you are essentially programming your mind to think and not just think at random but to think in an order for which you dictate.

I use morality, desire, intent and emotion. This process creates a cycle of refractive logical processive thought for which to pass the energy and restrict that energy to a cyclic form, which promotes a higher chance of the thought passing over the same synapses each time. The greater the restriction the greater elevation is with each cycle performed in thought through refraction. To simplify this, consider the use of 1+1=2 and every time you contemplate 1+1=2, those synapses gain a residual charge. If you desire to solve the equation, it will receive the energy from desire. If that desire is aligned with your intent, which is to produce accurate information it too will obtain more energy or at least not be impeded by it. If you are passionate about numbers, this thought receives emotional energy and elevation occurs.

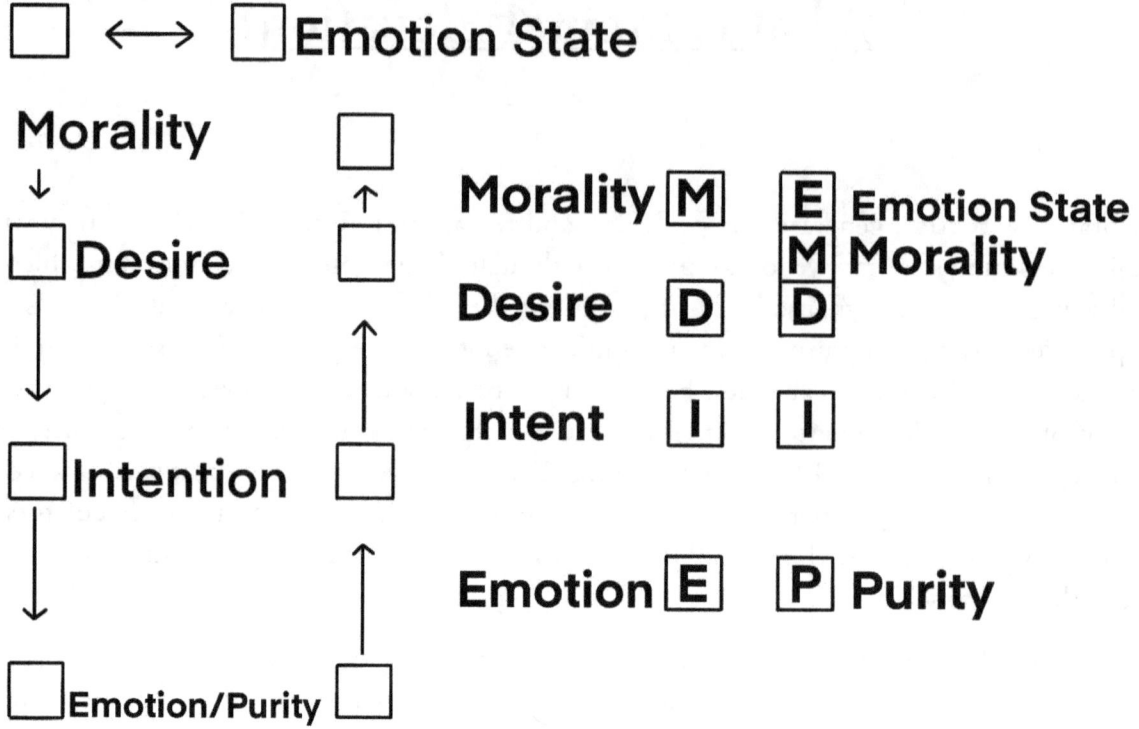

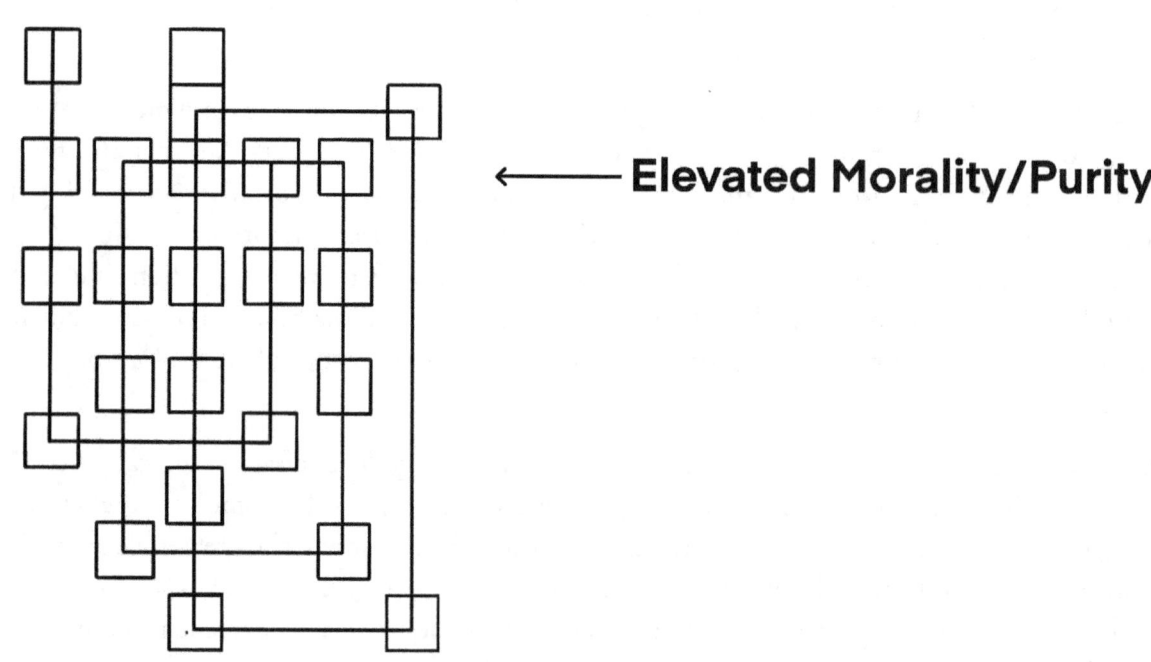

← Elevated Morality/Purity

How to ask for a Miracle?

In order to do this, you must first understand what this means, asking for a miracle is simply a request; just because you request it, this does not mean it shall be so or even that God said "no". What this means is you asked for something and it conflicted with the morality of God. God's morality is not just an inclusion of human life or any one species of life. It is literally an inclusive morality for all life and all things. Asking God to augment reality to satisfy a want or desire will result in rejection.

This does not mean you cannot ask for a miracle or that it will not be granted. This means it must abide by a set of conditions that do not cause conflict with the highest of all morality, sanctity and sanctuary for which the creator holds. This morality has solidified with the knowledge and experience of all in existence and that it has refined over billions, trillions, even zillions of years.

To begin, you must first reflect upon that which you ask; some basic things to consider during this reflection is how does this affect other life? How would this, if granted, affect reality itself? What negative conditions would granting this request bring forth? Reflection itself is essential as it will increase the possibility of success.

Consider the reality of what you are asking, take for instance, you asked to be able to move at the speed of light. If this was granted how dangerous would this be? Did you know that you're not aerodynamic and that if you take an object and go from point A to point B it would cause a collision with all the other particles between, projecting them by force at the speed of light away from it? If you move at the speed of light with a density value that collides with other particles with a near density, this occurs. Imagine crossing an ocean at or beyond the speed of light. The result would be destructive to far more than just humans. Superheating and producing a kinetic force through collisions that would create tidal waves, boiling and even vaporizing those nearby.

Asking for a miracle requires also for you to be devoid of self righteousness, devoid of greed, of self desire, of immorality altogether and there are several concepts to understand in this as well. When you ask for something like information, are you asking because you want to be famous? Do you want knowledge to get rich? Your request needs to be pure, you need to be pure. The purer the request, the greater the chance of it not just being heard but being granted. Your request should not be just for human benefit but for the benefit of all. With this said, you may be upset and not understand why it was not granted, but know that when you stand before the creator and ask why did you not grant my request? God will have your answer, as God's ability to educate is absolute and you will learn absolutely. Many misunderstand that even if you request it, you may be capable of fulfilling it yourself; thus, God will not. God may just tell you outright "be the miracle." God may have knowledge and understanding far beyond what you know at this time and it may be true that God can do so from scratch and you might never know the difference.

Those that purify themselves and fulfill these conditions may have their request not just heard but granted this Miracle by the Grace of God.

May God's light shine upon you all, in this life, and the next.

<u>The Third Eye</u>

Many folks talk about the use of the third eye; some talks revolve around the use of the pineal gland to activate such functions as astral projection and others talk about spiritual wellness or enhancing your self awareness, mental clarity and concentration. While these are all good things, some talk about what excessive negative energy can do; in some talks, this refers to obsession with psychic vision or could lead you to negative thinking and limited mental growth. Regardless of how this pineal gland is used or its functions within the realm of spiritual growth and awakening there is a scientific concept that is being ignored that should be explained. The eyes are a sensory organ that receives many different spectrums of light.

When your eyes are open, we receive the many particles of light you see everyday. Humans have 3 different types of cones that divide up the spectrum of our sight into red, green and blue. While the eye is open, it takes in the particles of light on a massive scale. You may not realize it, but a single light bulb produces tens of trillions of light particles if not hundreds. The light particles are bouncing all over the place, flooding our vision and illuminating the world around us.

What you may not realize also is that the eyelid has a function that acts like a filter; while the eye is open, the light is taken in at full capacity, massive amounts of particles pore into the eye and much like a very loud room where you attempt to hear the voice of someone next to you, your sensory organ is being flooded making it very difficult to isolate the desired information. While you can train your hearing to listen in the loud room to shut out the undesired noise, you do the same with your eye.

In order to use your eye this way apply your filter, biology provides you this filter as an eyelid, The eyelid itself removes massive amounts of excessive light particles naturally and this provides the sensor to be utilized much easier. So if you wish to see what is unseen or rather a light spectrum that requires a more sensitive receptor you should apply your natural filter. Close your eyes and allow the eyelid to remove the excessive light.

If you come across a form of light be aware that opening your eye will not make it go away, but it's a good idea to verify that it is not an afterimage, typically these after images move with the retinal focus and often occur when you stare at your lamp for a few seconds. Phosphene is a term that is often used to describe what occurs after a sneeze, cough or blow to the head. They typically appear as shapes, swiggles, swirls or dots.

While one concept refers to afterimages, another refers to shapes. The use of the eye's sensitive receptors is what you will use to observe the spiritual and is best done by applying your natural filter. Should you come across such an observation, ensure it does not follow your retinal focus, ensure that it was not because you stared at a light source and that you have not recently received a blow to the head or rubbed your eyes in some way. Try opening and closing your eyes, and move the retinal focus around the room; it should remain stationary and should you find yourself before an Eternal Spirit, be polite.

Beings of light and energy exist on a different density.

Parting Thoughts

Science and mathematical symbolism is not something to be in conflict with religious practices and is no different than the spoken word you use to educate others. It is an interpretation and a way to express that which you understand in a way others may then understand as well. While some choose to use the spoken word to educate, others use mathematical symbols to express that which is in our existence in a way their mind can understand and then share.

While one individual uses the spoken word to explain a phenomenon another uses symbols in the form of letters and numbers. This is done to create an organization of a phenomenon and while some have and may still attempt to classify this as some blasphemy it is not.

Just as the spoken word can be used immorally, so can science and mathematics. You can use language to do harm or to do good, which is true for science and mathematics as well. This is true, most notably in science and mathematical symbolism when considering the atomic bomb. I am absolutely certain Einstein did not intend for his signature to be used to create a weapon. The atomic bomb and its use does not just affect human life. It destroys all life and while human history reflects upon the loss of human life, understand that God reflects upon the loss of all life, not just human life.

The same can be done with spoken language and you can do harm in much the same way. In retrospect, the immorality resides within the intent. This is also notable when you swear; while it may be a vulgarity to do so, swearing is just a form of expression and to some, is perceived as immoral. While these are just spoken words, it is the expression and intent of its use that defines it.

Consider the intent for a moment of someone who is walking through their home and stubs their toe on the dining room table. The use of a cuss word, however vulgar in its usage to some, carries with it just an intent of extreme expression of pain and holds no direction towards another. When some feel pain, they often feel anger and so anger is expressed. While the use of the spoken word in this way is in some ways interpreted as immoral, the intent is not projected to do harm, nor is it used to express what some refer to as hatred.

Science and mathematical symbolism is in this way the exact same and it falls to the user to apply moral intent often referred to as ethics. Be ethical in your use of science, mathematics, religion and language. Manipulation using language is immoral and this includes pointing your finger at someone and telling them they are unworthy of God's love or that they will burn for eternity.

You do not command God's love.

Knowledge does not defy God's will.

It is not God's will that you remain ignorant.

PART 3:

The Science...

Formula for Peace on Earth

S(Ck x W)C=En|E=Peace on Earth

Is this Metaphorical, Philosophical or Literal-ism?

We first shall define particle progression: Particle progression, as defined by the frontal lobe as Physics, is the existence and presence that is an equal and unequal force that defines the result of an interaction using the calculations organized by source, result, positive and negative.

From Egyptian hieroglyphs to mathematical symbolism, and even all forms of language are simply frontal lobe tools to explain the known and unknown parts of reality. Just as Time is a measurement of particle progression in a way, the frontal lobe can then organize our daily lives. When you return to the origins of all of this, everything points to the source.

We will now use mathematical symbolism to define the peace on Earth formula:

When you understand that Will is a Bio-Energy and as it collides and charges synapses throughout the brain you receive a series of positive and negative interactions among the organic components. Taking this further and identifying the source of thought, this Bio-Energy as Will(W), we can focus this energy through our Cerebral Cortex(Ck) to another series of synapses and organic components to generate compassion for others which is Social Compassion (S) and (C), when this occurs within an individual's mind it becomes a series of (En) positive and (E)negative interactions through different organic components which are genetic memory structures programmed to function and complete various tasks in unison. The brain is capable of using cognitive De-Fusion and Re-Fusion to create Peace on Earth through the spread of True Acts of Kindness among your peers and over time, will breathe Humanity into the Cosmos. This is due to an organic component within the brain that controls Empathy.

Empathy: The ability to sense other people's emotions, coupled with the ability to imagine what someone else might be thinking or feeling. The ability to understand and share the feelings of another.

Will = W

Cerebral Cortex = Ck

Social Compassion = S and C

Positive = En

Negative = E

S(Ck x W)C=En|E=Peace on Earth

Particle Progression

Particle Progression

Author : Eric Kikkert

Originally Authored: January 1, 2020

Updated: April 28, 2024

Particle Progression

****

Affiliations:

U.S.Armed Forces-U.S. Army Aberdeen Proving Grounds Machinist Training Center 2004

Acknowledgment:

I acknowledge the many members of the world for their efforts to understand and better the future knowledge of humanity to include but not limited to, Aristotle, Newton, Pythagoras, Einstein, Stephen Hawking, Michio Kaku, Brain Cox, James Grime, as well as those responsible for research data listed below.

Keywords:

Quantum Relativity, Velocity, Particle Progression, Momentum, Entropy, Gravity

Abstract:

In this article I propose revisions to some basic functions to facilitate and detail an inclusive construct of calculation to remove the inability to define as a whole, that which is physics before and after "The Big Bang" or rather, "existence" before and after the emergence of energy and decay by creating a construct that can.

Opening Statement:

It is my hope that those who read this article do so with an open mind, for within it contains information that some may find controversial, if not provocative, to say the least, though it should at least in some meager sense prove to be enlightening if not inspiring. Further, it is my firm belief that it would, at minimum, be considered by Albert Einstein to be noteworthy and may, perhaps, even place a smile upon his face. If I am not mistaken, it was Socrates that stood before a jury in Athens. As the father of Greek philosophy, it was his belief that all things in life should be questioned. As such, he disputed anything that was widely considered to be true. With that, I too shall "Question Everything".

Introduction:

A basis to allow for the calculation of physics as it is before and after "The Big Bang" and provide a new understanding of the laws of physics and further the knowledge of humanity with this understanding. As we identify some concepts that currently prevent such logic and break down the basic revisions to remove and enable such calculations to include and logically permit its use with mathematical symbolism.

Question One:

What formulas and current mathematical logic prevents or deters the ability to apply constructs of physics to the conditions before "The Big Bang" or "emergence of energy and decay"?

Question two:

What revisions can we apply that would allow mathematical logic to calculate the before and after The Big Bang?

Research:

Research was conducted using an internet search to identify the use of formulas that derive conditions of time, velocity, gravity, momentum, entropy, particle physics. A vast majority of this was extracted from various Google searches under the above context and was detailed in a number of documents on basic physics. As a mechanical engineer the foreknowledge derived from military training and course work present during my service at U.S. Army Aberdeen Proving Grounds Machinist Training Center. Many concepts were extracted from Aristotle, Newton, Pythagoras, Einstein, Stephen Hawking, Michio Kaku, Brain Cox, James Grime.

(Due to copyright issues, the direct links are removed - conduct internet search of: Velocity, String Theory, Time, Momentum, Velocity, The Big Bang, weight, $E=mc^2$, Energy, Decay, Particle Wave Duality, Order of Operations, Density, Volume, Radial Curve, Thermal Dynamics.)

Hypothesis:

That it is possible to create using mathematical logic, a method to calculate, before and after "The Big Bang" or emergence of energy and decay.

Question One:

What formulas and current mathematical logic prevents or deters the ability to apply constructs of physics to the conditions before "The Big Bang" or "emergence of energy and decay"?

Answer To Question One:

The derived formulas that include conditions only usable for post Big Bang concepts are the issue. These formulas deter and inhibit an inclusion of mathematical logic that allows for the same calculations and mathematical logic to exist, and be used, before and after this event.

The basic formulas I found that exist after an internet search are conditionally including concepts of time, energy, velocity, momentum, matter, force, gravity, and entropy. The answer resides within the foundations for which these specific formulas exist.

The use of space-time conflicts with the ability to calculate using the same model of particle mechanics as defined by the emergence of energy and decay. Thus this emergence permits the use of a construct called "Time" to begin by providing the measurable concept of energy by its decaying properties. The use of Time is misconstrued to assume the ability of a forward and backward motion and to better facilitate this construct accurately, a proper term must be applied to remove misconceptions while including the ability to properly annotate the path of the particle in a progressive manner. This must be done because current physics defines the emergence of "Space-Time" and thus is incapable of being used to define a state before its emergence.

Several factors to understand that with this construct, there are no saved points to return to; existence is not storing that data and providing a point or means to access it. That the particle's forward progression remains true even if its trajectory is reversed using absolute control. That the use of force to return a set of particles to a previous location is not a reversal of "Time" but simply the continued forward motion whereby you have augmented the particle or sub-particles position and that the construct is still progressing forward by which the forward motion places those particles or sub-particles into a position that only emulates a previous state.

"The general view of physicists is that time started at a specific point about 13.8 billion years ago with "The Big Bang", when the entire universe suddenly expanded out of an infinitely hot, infinitely dense singularity, a point where the laws of physics as we understand them simply break down. This can be considered the "birth" of the universe and the beginning of time as we know it."

(Due to copyright issues, direct link is removed - conduct internet search: what is time and the big bang.)

"Velocity" uses the construct of acceleration, but since acceleration is a result and not a source, we must identify the source of "Velocity". The most direct condition of "Velocity" is "Force". Be it even the "Force" applied at creation and as such "Velocity" is calculated based on the "Density by Volume" to produce the variable result of "Velocity" and so it is identified as the result of "Force" applied to the calculation of "Volume by Density" we measure as "Weight". The source is identified as the "Volume and Density" and the result is defined or measured as "Weight" where "Force" is applied to create "Velocity".

As a condition of "Velocity" the use of "Time" is used and since before "The Big Bang" the use of "Time" to include by mathematical logic cannot be applied to a particle that would exist before its emergence. Hence, the use of "Time" in this calculation must be removed and instead "Progression" is applied.

"Momentum" uses a result and not a source to be defined. As the "density of its volume" and acceleration produce the result of force in the absence of additional force relative to the environment to which it exists. This momentum is a derived result of applied force. As such, the source must be used instead of the result. In basic terms, the momentum is a result of a force applied to a construct based on its "Density by Volume".

Weight is using a result of gravitational force between separate particles regardless of volume by density. We can observe these conditions between separate constructs and identify that both constructs do include a form of attraction. This attraction creates the result of weight defined by that density and volume. The most basic construct that defines this is present in tidal fluctuations as the Moon rotates around the Earth.

Entropy is a condition which, in most cases, disables the understanding of atomic and subatomic flow, "often interpreted as the degree of disorder or randomness of the system". Entropy itself is an unusable construct to create precise physics for which the inability to project or measure the "Trajectory and Velocity by its Volume of Density" is a result created from the lack of information. This lack of information may even be a result of the inability to measure those factors. As such, Entropy must be removed and a new construct which permits the absolute calculation should be used.

"The second law of thermodynamics says that entropy always increases with time" and "lack of order or predictably; gradual decline into disorder."

"a marketplace where entropy reigns supreme".

(Due to copyright issues, the direct link is removed - conduct internet search: Entropy.)

Considering two main factors by use of time and disorder, we lose the ability to include this with a before "The Big Bang" calculation. We must maintain the conditions of "Order" and the disuse of "Time". This also conflicts with by use of disorder or terms of chaos to obtain an absolute calculation. Such as the formula made by Stephen Hawking includes the use of Entropy.

Energy, as defined by Einstein, uses a function that is not associated as a source. The source is itself "Force", but is a result created and identified as "The Big Bang" calculations by use of "Mass or Matter" and Energy all of which are in fact a result of such "Force". With regards to $E=MC^2$ we see a use of the result of particles under a condition of higher "Density by Volume" (referred to as "Mass or Matter") which is converted to a representation of equal standing to its higher "Volume" less "Dense" state (referred to as "Energy"). Since "Mass or Matter" uses this result it cannot be included until after such an event occurs as seen with the emergence of energy referred to as "The Big Bang". As we backtrack through the creation process, it becomes clear that even energy becomes a result of force.

Even when considering string theory we come into a condition in which energy exists already and as such it does not permit the existence of such strings without the use of energy, since the emergence of energy has yet to occur strings therefore do not yet exist and "The Big Bang" may provide an explanation as to how such energy was created and tension between particles is now applied. In order to define how strings come into existence with an inclusive particle model, one must be able to use the same particle model to define even the birth of strings. Thus concluding by logic that strings are a result of the emergence of energy and we still must provide a logical construct and formula to be capable of calculating the existence of before and after. Thus, the creation of this article and the reason for which it exists.

Velocity

Momentum

Weight

Entropy

Energy

Question two:

What revision can we apply that would allow mathematical logic to calculate the before and after The Big Bang?

Answer To Question Two:

With the main formulas defined as conflicting with an inclusive definition and the mathematical logic of before and after the event, the following revisions can be applied to remove concepts that disassociate this inclusive model and mathematical logic.

In reference to string theory, it lacks the ability to define a state of existence without the use of energy and when presenting mathematical logic a particle model must be capable of defining a state of existence both before the existence of such energy as a lack thereof and with the existence of energy. It must be capable of being used regardless of how particle tension is defined and this requires a model that is expansive in this use and capable of being used in every form of logic that could exist. For even if we define its existence in another way or using something other than strings such as particle waves, the model must be inclusive in such a manner that it can with or without such uses be presented even to define the birth of strings.

Tools:

Since a current particle model does not permit the conditions of mathematical expression using logic as is with consideration to time, weight, velocity, momentum, energy. A new form of model must be derived.

This model is called particle progression and is using a method of calculation that removes any mathematical shortcuts further reducing all calculations based on a positive and negative interaction and by association of categories of source and result with the understanding that negative is the absence of the positive. This model does not incorporate the use of "Time" and instead uses a chronological statement of creation as a progressive factor in a step-by-step process used to identify a segment of existence for which decay had not yet existed. It holds no other limits. The following formulas were revised in application of such "Particle Progression".

The use of "Particle Progression" is needed because the creation of "Space-Time" had not yet begun and the ability to define this interaction requires a system of comparison for which to reference without decay using Force, Volume, and Density. To facilitate a direct model capable of mathematical logic before and after the existence of energy.

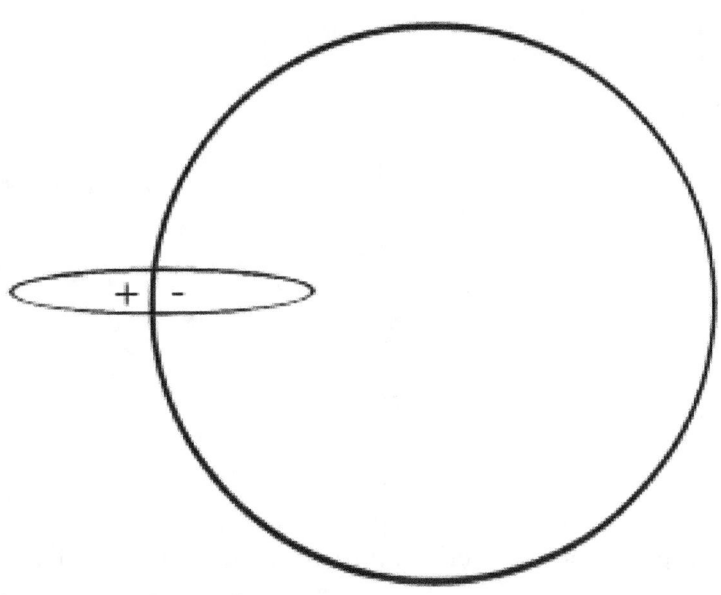

Velocity:

This is where we remove the use of the term "Time" and place "Progression". This is to better represent the chronological order of creation by the use of P instead of T in the following formula.

pos = s sine 4p

[-----------/

Where p = progression

S= 4 sine 4p

V= $\underline{ds}$ = 4 cosine 4p (4)
     dt

V(p) = 16 cosine 4p

-1 $\leq$ cosine 4p $\leq$ 1

1=16

Momentum:

This is revised to express the proper result by application of force as a positive and negative interaction. Done so to identify the source and the resulting momentum of such volumes of density.

It should read as follows:

That momentum is the progressionary derivative of force.

M x V = D x F = Momentum

Where M = Mass

Where V = Volume

Where D = Density

Where F = Force

Weight:

This is revised to better represent and associate values of the particles as a dual function of progressive pull and represent the tension between particles based on the "Density" values to produce proper calculations and express why light is affected by gravity and the tidal flow from the moon. By classifying proper electron residue to include sub-atomic particles. This can even be construed to represent how and why the construct of strings exist.

Er = Electron Residue

$$\frac{I \text{ Result} = R = \textbf{Weight}}{I}$$

Er = Density

x = Density x Gravity = R = Weight

ER = Gravity

E=MC²

This revision is to properly associate the source material (Density) and exclude the result (Mass) based on its "Density and Volume". As "Mass" or "M" is a result and the source is "Density" or "D" we identify that source based on the electron residue by "Density". Essentially we exclude the misconceptions of the sum by explicitly using the parts. Since our current algebraic functions require two parts to equal a sum, while reality does not it becomes a function in which an algebraic function fails to define properly and without the proper understanding that reality itself does not use algebraic functions to define itself and that it simply uses "Density by Volume" and that the term "Mass" is a man made concept to represent a sum of the parts physics begins to disassociate the structure of a particle such as light with any mass even though it should be included and expressed as a particle of such an extremely low density. We must in order to fully grasp the structure, calculate in the exact way it is in existence. In most cases even the use of "Order of Operations" distorts this in which we define that order by the observer and not by the phenomenon. This comes from "Order of Operations" defined as (Parentheses, Exponents, Multiplication, and Division (from left to right)), Addition and Subtraction (from left to right), under mathematical rules and is a distortion to the "Chronological Order of Creation" defined by the phenomenon itself. The observer is not to define the order of calculation.

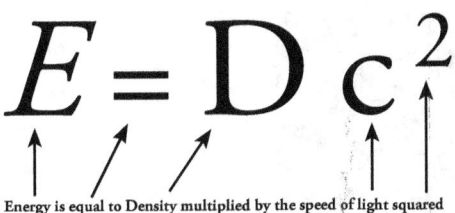

$$E = D\,c^2$$

Energy is equal to Density multiplied by the speed of light squared

Entropy:

This is revised to explain what is currently considered disorder or chaos as a "Progressional Order by Chronological Statement of Creation" using a 360 degree construct we refer to as Pi and is explicit for the definition of all particles and their perspective sub-particles trajectory within a variable of Pi. To best facilitate this and gain absolute precision a new method of calculation of the construct itself should be applied where all parts of the structure be converted to a whole number. Since the use of division presents problems when returning to the whole under a 360 degree calculation, we use a new form of representation by mapping the exterior and all interior parts by the segmented components based on the degree of accuracy we desire. Applying 4th dimensional positioning to represent the location within the construct we can then extrapolate its trajectory by including each factor and then determine its precise location within the structure at any progressional value. This will be essential to identifying the positions of subatomic particles and their trajectories could be used to plan the collision of such subatomic particles in particle colliders.

One such method is:

The concept is called the Pi Maker and it details how to reverse engineer a 360 degree circle into a segmentation of any value and convert those segments into a value of 1 to achieve a perfect circle or sphere. It is done by multiplication 360 x 114 = 41040 segments of 1 to obtain a complete and perfect circle or sphere.

Here is the basic concept:

360 - degrees of a circle = A

114 - segmentation value = B

41040 - equivalent of 360 degrees times the segmentation value = C

D = 12 inches

360 x 114 = 41040 x D = E

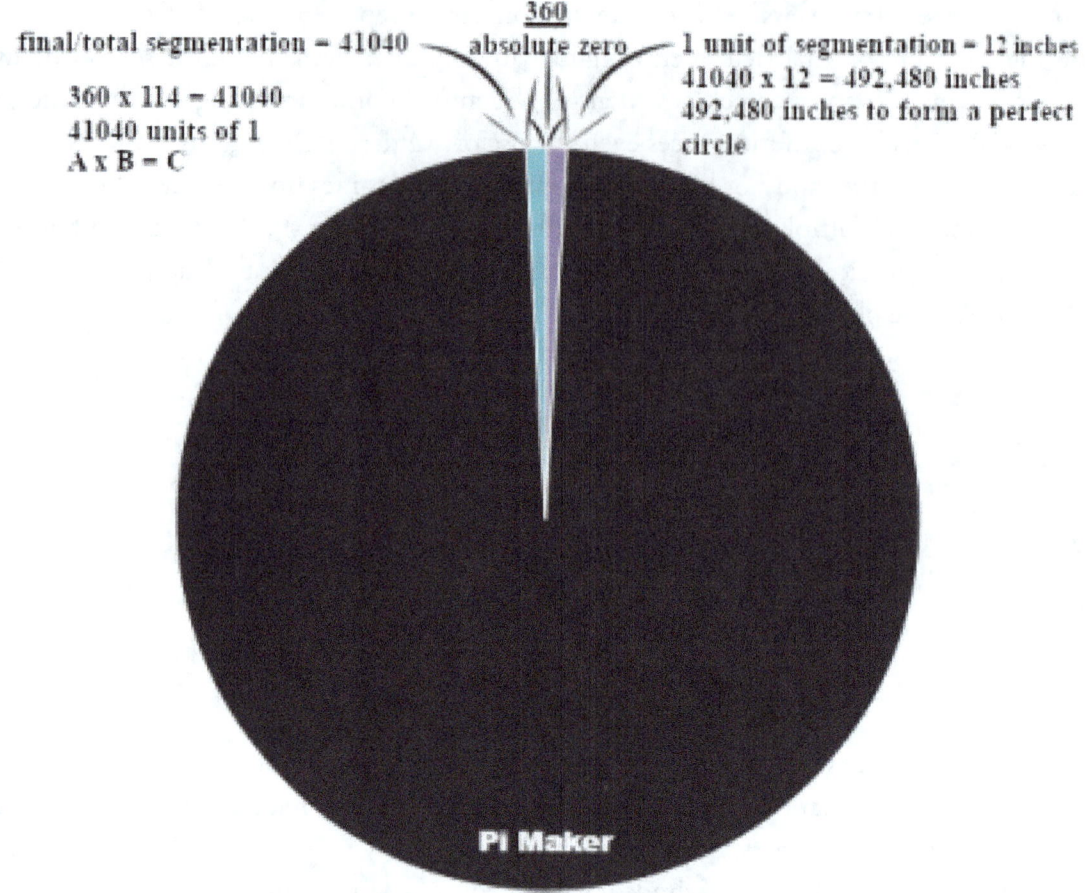

final/total segmentation = 41040

360
absolute zero

1 unit of segmentation = 12 inches

360 x 114 = 41040

41040 x 12 = 492,480 inches

41040 units of 1

492,480 inches to form a perfect

A x B = C

circle

Pi Maker

I have gone over a few ways to actually write this. But essentially, what this does is convert 360 degrees into a segmented value at 114 so that each segment, when multiplied together, becomes a whole number of 1, so 41040 (ones) makes the perfect and complete circle. Assigning as many perimeter values as needed and identifying segments of C as points of reference along simple or complex axes and the circumference. If you want more accuracy, increase the points of reference; just ensure that it remains a factor of C. In a quantum computer, this would permit complete mapping of the atomic flow along a series of these points.

When you complete this and include each segment of revision, you extract the results of quantum relativity. Where you can not only calculate the before and after "The Big Bang" using the same particle model of "Particle

Progression" but properly define the quantum explosion itself under "Progression-al Order by Pi". In the below formula, we see the use of a "Gravity Well Conversion" represented by (GWC) the result of extreme positive "Density" to create a gravity well as the Electrons condense and the resulting "Special Equivalent Atomic Exchange(SEAE)," which occurs as a result and the resulting modifications to Stephen Hawking's formula to remove "Entropy" and include "Progression-al Order by Pi(poPi)" as well as the revision to "E=MC2(E=DC2)" to also include the actual result of Pi which represents the quantum explosion which results by calculation as a representation of a spherical shape. This is a symbolic representation of the phenomenon itself and its components, which result from the quantum explosion created by the collision of force interlocked in force through either collision or compression. Understand this is interpreted by each component as a whole and not separate occurring parallel or simultaneously as a result from the source.

Where Entropy was S place poPi = progression-al order by Pi

Cosmic Alchemy = Spacial Equivalent Atomic Exchange (SEAE)

$$\frac{¥Akc3}{[---poPi---]} = ---q--- \quad \frac{SEAE}{[+/-]} = ---e--- \quad \frac{Pi}{E=M} = [E=MCPi]$$
$$2hG \qquad\qquad GWC$$

Conclusion:

In consideration and objective view of the above formula revisions it is my conclusion that it is entirely possible to create an inclusive and mathematically logical model of calculation to define both before and after the event we call "The Big Bang". Not only does this specific particle model "Particle Progression" encompass a series of particles, but can be applied to all particles regardless of what they are, under all forms of density and by any volume in any extreme condition or environment for which they exist.

The particle model called "Particle Progression" created from the revisions and logic present in this article allows for the ability to define physics as a whole by holding the ability to define before and after the emergence of energy. This includes the birth of strings themselves while also allowing for the mathematical logic to define any form of interaction between them and form of density by volume using positive and negative interactions by category of source and result. As the sources are identified and traced back to the origins, the source itself is defined by "Force".

"Thus, we exist because force exists. As such all things that exist are a result of force and the source of all is force."

In order to make a particle model that includes the existence of all under one it must be capable of detailing all that exists and be capable of when all that exists did not exist. This is how we obtain the understanding using mathematical logic as an all-inclusive model to detail everything that exists and using the same model to detail when it did not.

This model holds one downside as it would not incorporate mathematical logic to define an existence without a positive and negative, such as positive only. Thus, we define this condition as a void of null density whereby only one conditional density resides and is referred to as null or "Void of Null Density". Under this, we can extrapolate that in such a condition of null, all was if even for a single moment one and without a comparison to determine a variable of measurement would effectively be today considered zero.

Under this condition of null, if you compressed null by volume you would gain the effect of positive and negative by reducing a volume null to create an alteration of its density to be greater and the volume is less. As the extreme of this condition persists to compress, we obtain a notable source of force by expansion back to null from a compressed state whereby force has compressed and then expanded to generate a condition of extreme force relativistic in a state of existence in which null resides, any application of force becomes extreme. By which from nothing we obtain something. Since this model is capable of detailing the force from a void and variant of such density, it persists to allow and include an existence of such with and without the use of particle energy, tension, momentum, weight, velocity, strings, or matter regardless of what they are or how they interact and even how they are created.

Further extrapolation of variants, particle progression, allows density to density and also volume to volume; if the density to density is different, it persists as a variant of comparison and thus identified. If volume to volume is different, this also defines a comparison between each and also persists, meaning that even if space as it is now is compressed, it can be identified and measured as such under mathematical logic, the conditions in which it cannot define is when all conditions are exactly the same density and no volume exists. It is my understanding that the void of null density is where of-like coagulation occurs and force is first applied, giving rise to variants even through the interlocking of force within force itself. That the collision and resulting rupture of this interlocked force creates the kinetic force to create energy.

Even in reference to Nikola Tesla in depiction of energy as a vibration and frequency, these are results and conditions of measurement by which the source of interlocked force resides within a determined space with a specific density. If we referred to the atomic particle and define the reference of how these frequencies and vibrations are created, we would perceive a battery as the Protons are positively charged particles, neutrons are uncharged (negative) particles with orbital atomic particles as electrons and this would identify closely as a back emf switch at the sub atomic level producing the frequency and vibration through electron orbits which we measure as by the speed or velocity for which the orbits occur as the energy created defines or produces vibrations in interval referred to as frequency.

Conditionally verified by super cooling the system and observing the modifications. This interlocked force defines how strings are created and other binding forms through the electron residue, though considering the conditions of electron residue as the source of energy in reference to the string's electromagnetic force, which creates the tension is still a representation of a result and not the source. Even calling them strings is a bit of a stretch, as electron residue interactions resemble more like "Wi-Fi" where it connects in a radius of the field to all, of-like particles more closely represented to that of a sphere. While these fields are composed of particles, they could be presented as a string, but it would not be defined as a single string but a vast number, far greater than anyone would care to count, up to any number defined by the capacity of the source energy based on a value of the circumference. Just as lightning is made up of many particles, so too is the string.

Remembering that from space, the oceans appear as waves upon the shores, the reality of it exists as particles of water collected together which form the wave; this is a general function that identifies particle wave theory itself. These waves of energy are actually countless particles of a volume beyond our ability to isolate individually; just as a single photon can be identified, all particles of energy function in the same manner. This can be detailed by absorption rates, refraction and many other forms of interactions these waves perform, this includes radiation. Currently, we may lack the visual prowess, and sensitive tools to measure them for documentation.

Conditions of particle waves and the conditions of duality are defined by density; if you consider a particle of low density such as energy, a few things may occur based on this density.

First, the particle of energy expands without an increase in density or charge and would then be spread over an area as an expanded construct since segmentation of the particle becomes identified based on the charge within the density by volume, the transmitter and the condition identified by the receiving surface or component, and energy of two types intermix to become one, the defined particle as it expands is then partitioned as that segment of density by volume is interacted or absorbed.

The second is that the particle of energy is transmitted with an increase in density determined by the force of charge and spreads multitudes of the whole particle into a refractive form, just as the water molecules act in an oceanic wave.

Third, these extremely low density particles are extremely sensitive to outside influences that includes absorption by the retina. Other energy particles may collide with constricting the flow of the particle, but if they are of a different type will not intermix; this includes other weaker forms of electromagnetic energy of any type, including ones produced by humans. These conditions seem to baffle present scientists, but the conditions that define each and every particle regardless of its expanded higher volume lower density state or its lower volume higher density state.

Fourth, Particle Collision occurs when two particles of the same type collide, while they can intermix and become as one, they can also separate and even partition and essentially scatter, this would be a dispersal of the base particle. It also occurs in high variation depending on velocity and momentum, which is directly correlated to the density by volume. They may join and proceed on the same course or refract off each other depending on the amount of force applied. This can be easily defined by water droplets as they closely resemble the base function. When considering Particle Collision, you must also take into consideration the density of the absorbing material, as most materials do contain many internal angles and chasms internally and on its surface, these structures alter and change the refraction trajectory of the particles and also permit its absorption. While absorption transference does occur, particularly in glass, other materials will not. So, with Particle Collision, we will see a large variance in the output, this can even occur with partial collision, just as two people walking into each other would. Some may collide and hold each other and some may ricochet at different points, center and off center for instance, even grazing blows. Since the density, velocity, volume, momentum and type are factors it becomes difficult to predict at a distance. This is where progressional order by pi is used.

A practical way to explain this is to consider the particle, and the interior of that particle is at a set volume with a density of 0.1 and the space outside that particle is 0.000001. As force is applied in an expansive trajectory outwards, much like a quantum explosion, the exterior density would perceive the interior as quite solid in comparison; as this expansion occurs, the interior density, or shell of the photon, would push outwards, decreasing the interior density but increasing its volume, the exterior density would increase due to spatial atomic equivalent exchange based on space, force, and density, this function when applied to the creation of space, as we know it today, is defined by the extreme force used in its creation which being one of the only infinite constructs that exist can modify any density as long as enough force is used, at some point force exceeds any condition of density or rather, force itself can dictate the existence any density. If the force creating the expansion is raw kinetic force or rather not energy or force of the same type as the particle, the shell will stretch instead of assimilating the particles into the shell during expansion; consider this process to include the tension between the particles.

When regarding the conditions of what specifically generates the first creation of any electrons, be it by particle collision, compression, the initial burst of energy created from the collision and/or rupture of interlocked force, or even by the combination of particle collision and compression in conjunction with the the rupture of interlocked force which suggests the creation of the electron and then the slow decay of those electrons to create residue. This formula and its basic structure includes any and all forms of these creation methods. As read in a new scientific article that identified photonic collisions can and do create electrons, it can still be used to define and detail either method; the issue required to determine is which came first, photon or electron. This will provide the exact chronological order of creation. In either case the same construct can define and be used for both to create the mathematical method of logic and a universal construct to use with and without the existence of energy.

Final thoughts:

After going through each set of formulas used, the basic understandings therein, many of the terms used to identify these constructs are in part or as a whole misconstrued and create misconceptions, in science itself, it is best to gain absolute precision in both mathematical representations and the explanations and so many of the terms used, the structures present, we have broad definitions that allow for these misunderstandings and lack of precise definitions specifically placed in the many meanings of the terms themselves. This inhibits our progress forward and further complicates the ability for these constructs to be handed down to younger generations without vast amounts of explanations. Such is a construct we refer to as "TIME", this construct which is vastly misunderstood. It is a means by which the human mind can organize our daily lives. It itself, as we understand it, does not actually physically exist. It is a term widely thought about and is best represented by the term "Progression" for this structure removes the misconception placed in today's term of "Time". The collision of particles and energy, the decay of those particles from external or internal sources is what we identify.

The use of "Density" is also vastly misunderstood. Every particle that exists does, in fact contain a density and this density is the reason for which we determine other factors to include light speed. These density values are in present science, difficult to measure but not impossible to do so because these "Density" values are at such an extreme their own creation generates the force required for it to obtain what we consider maximum velocity, that maximum "Velocity" is not a "Constant". The application of additional force will push that particle beyond its perceived maximum we refer to as "Constant". The "Constant" terminology is only applicable to a particle without additional force or external influence and resistance. Through its initial creation, the density of the light particle is at such an extreme that the application of any force whatsoever produces what we consider as light speed to occur. That should these particles be created without such force applied, they would, in fact, stand still.

This is prevalent when considering a void of null density or the creation of light with balanced force applied externally, even through its creation. In most cases present, we see a radiating construct that does, in fact, project these extreme low density particles outward. There are so many structures that exist that produce even the tiniest of forces, yet when we consider the creation of the first structures of these low density particles, it may not have had any force applied in this way. It may have actually been either created from scratch and that in this way, no external influence is applied so that this extremely low density particle received no force to propel it at all, leaving light sitting still where it was born.

One concept to consider, which may allude many for quite some time still, is the concept of spatial compression and how this leads to a step by step process to create energy, this process begins with a volume, which we refer as space, in this volume we have a density value, this density is augmented through spatial compression, creating diversity. Through that spatial compression, we identify an application of force which originates from the vast volume of this density. So, by using logic, we can determine that volume is first, then density is second, and force is third. You cannot have a density without a volume for it to exist, you cannot have a density without a volume, the density of that volume applies force through spatial compression.

Spatial Compression is the most notable concept for which force is applied through collective weight and as such, this generates the force that produces variants of density by volume and where we see a mathematical anomaly of Zero becoming One. This would be considered the first measurable condition of positive and negative interactions where a volume of the "VOID of Null Density" is reduced to create a variation of density. This interaction is the birth of our reality. In truth, "The Big Bang" itself is a result and though it may be the source of many things, it remains by all logic to be the result of "Force".

Comments:

In order to create a greater understanding of existence, physics, biology, philosophy and mathematics, it is highly advised to begin requiring the individuals to create a process to digest the phenomenon and break it down into its many components while including as many details as possible, then have each individual produce from scratch the formula using mathematical symbolism to explain and calculate its physics from scratch. Then compare it with what is known. The difference in this will be clear: one simply understands how to calculate Velocity. The other knows how to create a calculation of Velocity from nothing.

It is also highly likely that through interlocking force within force and a rupture of that force creates the first kinetic force to generate energy, produced from spatial compression, this compression then leads to the creation of the photon, which would create the electron. In the future, in order to complete certain functions in calculation, we will most likely need to begin using Baker's calculations (think about Babylon) as these fit uniformly into time, feet, degrees, etc. This allows for precise conversions and segmentation values. Where each unit of 1 is containing 12 sub units instead of 10, so we begin the count at one and end at twelve and this is 1 whole number.

Ultimately, everyone should consider using a uniformed and interchangeable unit of measure globally; this includes basic arithmetic. If you had done so originally and were raised from birth under the concept of 12 units per 1 whole number, the concept would be no different than using degrees, feet or time. Consider the fact that if all arithmetic was originally designed from scratch to be uniformed with every other form of calculation regardless of the form, we would not have nearly as many issues with conversions or segmentations.

I will give science a bit more time to define the 2 slit experiment and if still unable then I will educate.

"Education is not the learning of facts, but the training of the mind to think." Albert Einstein

"Intelligence is not the remembering of facts but the ability to think. To create from scratch the laws of physics itself will provide the deepest understanding of that which is." Eric J. Kikkert

For simplicity sake here is an easy to use conversion and even a nursery rhyme that can be used to help people learn.

M is to D as T is to P.

Where M is Mass.

Where D is Density.

Where T is Time.

Where P is Progression.

-quick reference:

M is to D as T is to P, we all fly free when we use density.

Short Communication
Volume 7:11, 2022

Journal of Infectious Diseases and Medicine

ISSN: 2576-1420

Open Access

How to Create Effective Vaccines

Eric Kikkert*

Department of Infectious Diseases, Church of Humanity, USA

Short Communication

You use a series of methods to dismantle the organism and prepare it for the bodies immune system.

Let's begin: The Slammer Method

First you place the organism itself inside your safe container. This container will be depressurized to implode the organism, next you will pressurize the organism to the extreme so that you crush every part of it, this container is then heated to an extreme and then also cooled to an extreme to produce the organism's chemical compounds without the organic structure intact. There are standards of extremes for each, such as the max temperature to use. You do not want to release any particles from the contained virus. The basics of this method is to prepare the organic structure of the virus to be fed to the white blood cell like a baby bird. Just as Anthrax is destroyed by the acids of the Hyena. While some organism do hibernate or go into stasis, they may still be dissolved.

You find the limits of each extreme in pressure, heat, cold and then match the host's white blood cells chemical dissolvent, while ensuring it cannot reproduce. I want to emphasize the fact your just feeding the white blood cell. This is then dissolved using the same chemical equivalent that the white blood cell (for all creatures to include animals) uses to break down organisms (enzyme) to create the vaccine which will allow the body to absorb it, giving the natural immunity the chemical id. The white blood cells are also food for some organisms so to verify we use basic methods already known to our medical teams today. The vaccine to be tested, should be placed and verified by direct food and reproduction stimuli.

If it can still eat or reproduce you did not do one of the following take away enough pressure, apply enough pressure, use enough heat, use enough cold, intoxicate or inhibit (if the organism ceases to function from pressure alone this is administered to the enzyme). Various things such as light are also effective, electricity, draining the energy from the organism yourself to include over working it (exhaustion and starvation), sound even, intense vibrations to include intoxication of the organism to inhibit reproduction or even eating, seeing, feeling, smelling, such as feeding it a chemical equivalent of caffeine to remove or inhibit the desire to feed. Analyzing the responses to the stimuli and chemical changes will give you the ability to cross reference the entire known chemical database against all known organism.

Remember that the chemical marker for the white bloods cells to register it as a target are present already. Consider a organism that fails to ingest or get ingested, these particles are not forever stuck in the body, all these fluids get removed the same way. Even the chemical marker used to engage the initial white blood cell, the presence of foreign objects of all kinds are broken down and dissolved. We simply need to hand it back to the body. Understand that when using this method we are including the entire construct as a whole and that there is a difference between the chemical compilation of a selected protein and the chemical compilation of the entire organism. Single protein vaccines are missing some of the following parts of the construct: Nucleocapsid protein, envelope, membrane and any other proteins available not present. Using each of these together will provide us the greatest result from our vaccine [1-5].

Conflict of Interest

None.

References

1. Rashi, Tsurel. "The moral and religious obligation to vaccinate children in Jewish ethics." Acta Paediatr 110 (2021): 2984-2987.

2. Hostler, Thomas J., Chantelle Wood and Christopher J. Armitage. "The influence of emotional cues on prospective memory: A systematic review with meta-analyses." Cogn Emot 32 (2018): 1578-1596.

3. Sato, Ryoko and Benjamin Fintan. "Fear, knowledge, and vaccination behaviors among women in Northern Nigeria." Hum Vaccin Immunother 16 (2020): 2438-2446.

4. Rus, Meta, and Urh Grošelj. "Ethics of vaccination in childhood—A framework based on the four principles of biomedical ethics." Vaccines 9 (2021): 113.

5. Baden, Lindsey R., Hana M. El Sahly, Brandon Essink, Karen Kotloff, Sharon Frey, Rick Novak, David Diemert et al. "Efficacy and safety of the mRNA-1273 SARS-CoV-2 vaccine." N Engl J Med (2020).

How to cite this article: Kikkert, Eric. "How to Create Effective Vaccines." J Infect Dis Med 7 (2022): 264.

*Address for Correspondence: Eric Kikkert, Department of Infectious Diseases, Church of Humanity, USA; E-mail: kikkerteric@icloud.com

Date of submission: 20 October, 2022, Manuscript No. jdm-22-77840; Editor Assigned: 22 October, 2022, PreQC No. P-77840; Reviewed: 05 November, 2022, QC No. Q-77840; Revised: 11 November, 2022, Manuscript No. R-77840; Published: 19 November, 2022, DOI: 10.37421/2576-1420.2022.7.264

ejbps, 2023, Volume 10, Issue 7, 50-51.

Research Article

SJIF Impact Factor 6.044

EUROPEAN JOURNAL OF BIOMEDICAL AND PHARMACEUTICAL SCIENCES

http://www.ejbps.com

ISSN 2349-8870
Volume: 10
Issue: 7
50-51
Year: 2023

THE LAZARUS PIT

Eric Jesse Kikkert*

U. S. Armed Forces-U.S. Army Aberdeen Proving Grounds Machinist Training Center 2004, 2201 Aberdeen Boulevard, Aberdeen Proving Ground, MD, United States. 21005-0000.

*Corresponding Author: Eric Jesse Kikkert
U. S. Armed Forces-U.S. Army Aberdeen Proving Grounds Machinist Training Center 2004, 2201 Aberdeen Boulevard, Aberdeen Proving Ground, MD, United States. 21005-0000.

Article Received on 21/05/2023   Article Revised on 11/06/2023   Article Accepted on 01/07/2023

ABSTRACT

This is designed as an alternative "method of treatment" to incorporate all forms of particle physicsusing the particle model called particle progression and cellular biology as a quantum structure in aprocess of reverse engineering mitosis to produce a highly effective treatment and alternative to chemotherapy and hyperbaric for cancer and other forms of cellular degeneration as well as promote viable solutions for other conditions presented such as cellular fatigue, weakened immune health.

KEYWORDS: Cancer, Mitosis, Treatment, Cellular Fatigue, Hyperbaric.

MATERIALS

Ozonator is used as a method to produce high levels of Oxygen and is present in commercial and non-commercial use.

Perfluorocarbon is used in liquid breathing in most general respiratory surgeries.

Hot-Tub is in general use to contain the liquid and provide an environment for which an individual may rest.

Earth Battery in this article is detailed as a ground generator of electricity which biodegraded compost provides, made by M. Emme in 1893 No. 495,582.

METHOD

The Lazarus Pit is designed to be used in conjunction with a mineral, vitamin and antioxidant smoothie to promote effective conditions for immune health while providing proper particle and energy transfer.

We begin with the base of a hot-tub, this hot-tub, uses fluid capable of holding extreme amounts of oxygen as seen in "Liquid Breathing".

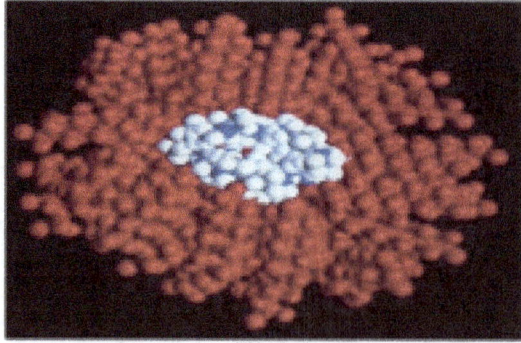

Fig. 1.

This fluid is used inside of the hot-tub and proliferated by using oxygenators often referred to as Ozonator. This will create micro bubbles of oxygen increasing and maximizing the oxygen levels in the fluid present in the hot tub for absorption. If you cannot obtain the carbon molecule it is permitted to use alkaline water, do not use the hot tub chemicals this will deter the cleansing process as they are absorbed by the body, instead drain every few days and wash the container with dawn soap. Then refill.

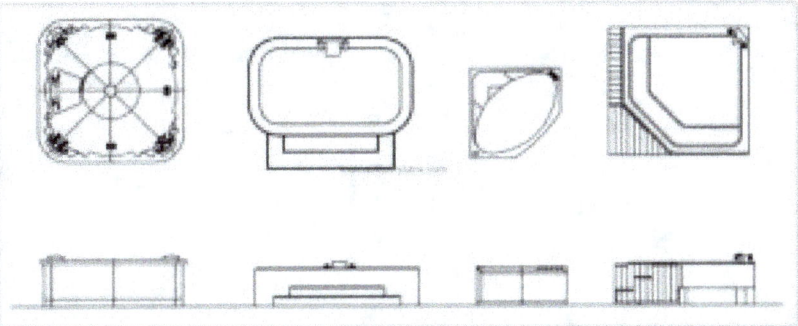

Fig. 2.

This will be connected to a compost of decaying materials such as vegetation, the vegetation will decay and be connected to channel the decayed energy into the fluid we will call the earth battery. This will provide the body with ample natural energy. This decayed energy produced will give fatigued cells the ability to utilize and absorb energy required to produce proper mitosis of the cells at a micro-biological level. This earth battery will be placed into the center of the decayed compost system. Then connected using conductive material in a protective shell to prevent unwanted displacement of energy while permitting transfer into the fluid within the hot-tub.

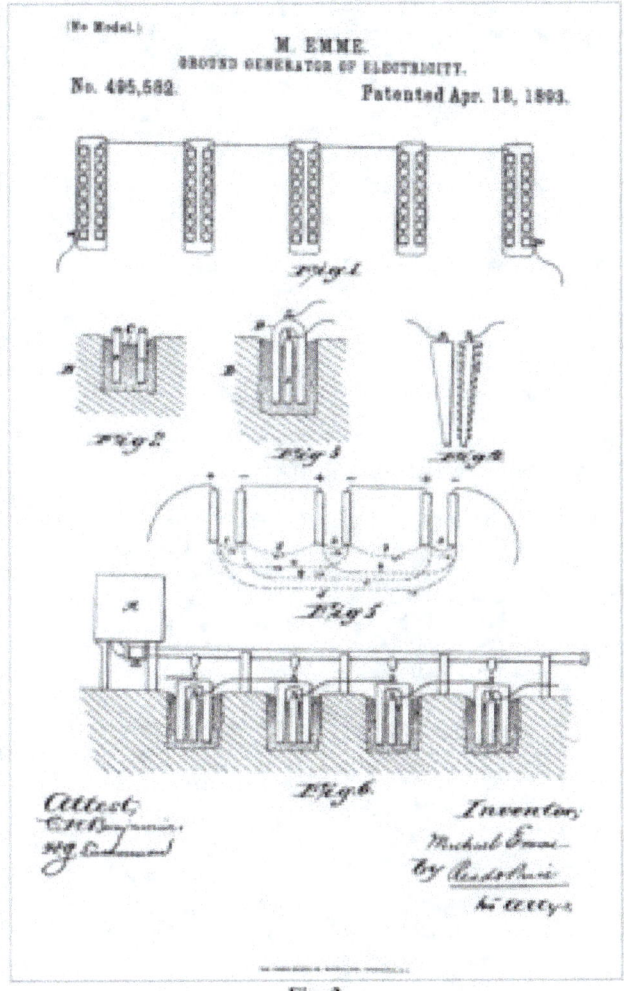

Fig. 3.

56

Eric *et al.*   European Journal of Biomedical and Pharmaceutical Sciences

When combined with the high-capacity oxygenated liquid and the use of the smoothie, we provide for the body and proper conditions, particles and energy needed for proper immune and cellular mitosis.

What foods help remove conditions of cellular irregularities:

First let's understand that an increase in lactate and decrease in oxygen levels increase the irregular growths and in order to provide an optimal condition for the body to correct this we can use food intake.

Increasing probiotics for bowel health with carrot, salt and vinegar in an alkaline based water with baking soda and fruit smoothie: (lactates provide cells such as cancer an optimal environment for reproduction reducing lactate in the blood is vital)

Uses of anti-lactate plants such as: (use of vitamin E reduces collagen linking and production by reducing the break down of unsaturated fats).

Consider cardiovascular workout to open the capillaries and increased blood flow. Just enough to promote regulatory blood flow, increase body temperature.

Baking soda
1 gallon of water a day (Alkaline)
Bell peppers (Red and Yellow) Black Currant Green beans Potatoes Berries Kidney Beans Walnuts

Use of plants and fruit to provide oxygen transfer and production: (clogged lungs decrease oxygen levels in the blood) smoking and asbestos where fibers clog the lungs and prevent oxygenation.

Lemons (Reduces Lactate and Improves oxygen)
Avocado, Berries, Carrots, Ripe Bananas, Celery, Broccoli, Garlic, Dates, Alfalfa Sprouts, Apricots, Sweet Apples, Sweet Grapes, Pears, Passion Fruit, Raisins, Chicory, Asparagus, Watercress, Seaweed, Parsley, Papaya, Limes, Melons, Kiwi, Cantaloupe, Mango, Peaches, Pineapple, Oranges.

Drinking a smoothie made from these will have a tremendous homeopathic treatment which will lead to recovery and is a verified method to combat irregularities in cell growth, promote immune health and proper mitosis.

DISCUSSION
- Kay factors that may cause mitosis to occur with disorder
- Dehydration: Lack of space to preform mitosis.
- Blood clots: Reduced volume of required free space for mitosis to occur.
- Lack of particles: Lack of nutrients equates to lack of particles to supply and preform. Minerals or vitamins. This lack of particles cause a deficiency in the mitosis process.

- Lack of energy: During the decomposition of food particles the decayed bio energy is transferred into the body through biodegradable process preformed by the stomach and intestines. This even equates a lack of energy causing cellular fatigue which prevents proper force to be applied during mitosis.

Toxicity levels: Toxins accumulate within the body to prevent proper mitosis from occurring. These toxins reduce the ability to absorb nutrients and transfer energy as particles and when considered to be a atmospheric condition of the cell, all respective conditions become factors or determining conditions for particle and energy transfer.

Lack of oxygen: the lack of oxygen is a key promotion to irregular mitosis and prevents the regenerative abilities and lowers overall immune health.

RESULT
The result of this method will be to provide in every possible way all the particle values by reverse engineering of the mitosis process to incorporate physics and particle progression to create an ideal condition of mitosis and deter the irregular mitosis by supplying both a pristine condition withample energy, proteins, minerals and vitamins.

One of the key factors that is provided by The Lazarus Pit, is the external source of natural energy through biodegradation which replicates the stomachs digestive process and provides vast amounts of oxygen, proteins, minerals and vitamins.

Another factor to The Lazarus Pit is oxygenation of the body to promote immune health as an alternative to hyperbaric.

CONCLUSION
Considering the introduction of particle progression as a universal method in quantum relativity and mechanics is relatively new, a deeper dive into The Lazarus Pit and it's potential use for bio regeneration as applicable from a general standpoint, research and exploration into this new and potentially useful alternative method of treatment should be conducted. It is my conclusion that this method has the potential to cure a vast majority of ailments and cancers.

ACKNOWLEDGMENT
I acknowledge the many works of Ray Peat for their details into mitosis and immune health. To Albert Einstein for the quote "Question Everything". To European Journal of Biomedical and Pharmaceutical Sciences for consideration of the article. To M. Emme for the design of the Earth Battery patent listed. To my one true love for whom is my motivation and energy to make this world a better place.

Eric *et al.* European Journal of Biomedical and Pharmaceutical Sciences

REFERENCES
1. https://raypeat.com/ Patents:
2. M. Emme in U.S., 1893; 495: 582.
3. https://raypeat.com/ Chemical Terminology.
4. Perfluorocarbon.
5. Perfluorochemicals are chemically inert synthetic molecules that consist primarily of carbon and fluorine atoms, and are clear, colourless liquids. They have the ability to physically dissolve significant quantities of many gases including oxygen and carbon dioxide.

Semantic and Scientific Shifts

Semantic change refers to a type of language change in which the meaning of a word changes over time. Scientific definitions are also subject to change much the same way.

Narrowing is when a word's meaning becomes more specialized in time.

Broadening is when a word becomes more generalized and gains additional meanings.

Amelioration is when a word's meaning changes from negative to positive.

Pejoration is when a word's meaning changes from positive to negative.

Semantic reclamation is a process where a word that was once used to disparage a group of people is reclaimed by the group.

Regardless of how or why these changes occur it stands true that these modifications create distortions in what is written, as it is written today. So be aware of this and with each generation, ensure the use of the proper usages. Take note that when it occurs, it may occur for the sole purpose of manipulation of your understanding of what is written in the hopes you will be unable to fully grasp the meanings as they are intended.

A dictionary using the semantics as defined in the year 2020 and the language of English used by the United States of America.

Awesome and awful are the words derived from owe. Awesome means excellent, but awful means really bad. Formerly, awesome and awful were synonymous but at the end of the 19th century, the meaning of awful changed to extremely bad and frightful. In old English, awe meant dread, fear, and terror.

The meaning of SYNONYM is one of two or more words or expressions of the same language that have the same or nearly the same meaning in some or all senses.

Take into consideration that while the semantics of what is written may change, my use of it will not. As the language is modified my use in this writing will not. The same can be used to express scientific knowledge, such as the use of science to define life. It may be defined at another time to refer to organisms that do not display consciousness to mean they are not considered life and may attempt to refer to them as organic machines. This is not my intent, nor is it proper. Simply put, in this writing, life includes all forms of life, even those not presently known, such as life forms composed of energy. While the scope of science may currently fail to grasp life in its entirety or the density for which it may exist, it is true science uses only its current, comparable information for which it measures.

The depths to which life can and does exist is so vast you could not speak the names of these life forms even if you took your entire lifetime to do so and did nothing else.

How Existence Calculates

This knowledge is probably tens of thousands of years ahead of you so I do not expect anyone to truly understand it, regardless, here you go.

Existence is calculated on a system using only the whole number, and by comparison, all that exists beyond, even our known cosmos, is included. This means that all that exists, by any comparison, is at an integer value of one based on its density, and its volume is at the highest possible integer.

If you put this in simple terms by any comparable form, it would mean under standard system that each volume would be compared to the volume of existence. Which we could summarize as considerable to something far beyond googolplex to the power of a googolplex.

Since all integer values are of a whole, the density of this volume would then be represented by the integer value of 1. This is because it is of the highest volume at the lowest density.

Every volume of density is then compared to these values and falls within that relative range. Physics will take a considerable amount of time to grasp this concept, and you can traverse the cosmos. Understandably, even the most extremely advanced species would barely grasp the reality of this concept. That does not mean that we can not or that they can not. Clearly, it is comprehensible by the human mind for I have already done it. But this concept, as with many others, may be beyond most that exist.

Which is understandable; it is ok. It is ok for you to not grasp the reality of this yet, or even at all in the future. But this is how reality works, and it is how the system functions regardless of how you think it works.

When you break down the phenomenon known as existence as a whole and create physics literally as reality does, this is what you get. Mathematics itself, in terms of spatial calculations, holds no value of Zero. All things, including what you currently consider to be space, are not Zero. There is no Zero in spatial mechanics. There is always a value of the positive, and it is required to be fully calculated, as it calculates itself using the whole by comparison.

So if a googolplex to the power of a googolplex is the value of all in existence, and space is but a small portion of that integer, by comparison, the density and volumes that exist slide along that scale all the way beyond the atomic level many times over. Otherwise, everything you produce distorts reality and is merely an interpretation of this. An interpretation that is easier to organize and understand for the human mind. One day, we will be able to fully utilize this, and the true reality of quantum will be understood. Until then you have yet to fully grasp that which is quantum mechanics.

About the Author

Eric was born and raised in the United States of America, where he currently resides. Eric has taken many paths to define himself, he began his life as a metallurgist when he was 16, he became a bladesmith where he then went on to become a certified welder and later a machinist in the United States Army. He is a 5th generation Army Veteran, while in the army he served a tour in Iraq. Since his family has for many generations served in the military he was endowed with a higher sense of morality which was further influenced by his service to his country.

After his service he went on to become a state Certified Building Inspector for Lead Asbestos and Mold, it was shortly after this that Eric began his journey into the fields of Physics, mathematics, and biology in which he discovered and produced several new technologies, one such technology was a universal vaccine method, and also an alternative treatment of cancer, in which he was asked to present his work at a medical confrence in London. Both of these methods and new technologies are present in this book.

Eric has taken writing classes on the Hero's Journey in which he enjoyed thoroughly, while he enjoyed the learning process it became clear his true gift was not meant to just create stories but to define gifts which make the world a better place for all that exist. His experiences took on a whole new meaning when he began exploring the divine, through this discovery he found such truths that he felt the world should know. This gave rise to the foundations of this book and the reasons in which it was written.

Several of his favorite quote are:

"Physics makes your biology from scratch"

"Open your heart and your mind will follow"

"One does not do good for God, one does because it is righteousness. One does not, for reward of salvation or even for immortality, one does not do, for eternity. One does because it comes from the soul. "To Be" your true self, seek no reward."

"Within thy soul, a hero's light, flows with all, true loves might."